Salt Water Taffy Collection

Devoted to preserving heirloom quality in quilts and accessories, Rebekah Shucksmith shares her lifelong experience in English paper piecing, hand embroidery, and hand buttonhole stitch appliqué.

LEISURE ARTS, INC. • Maumelle, Arkansas

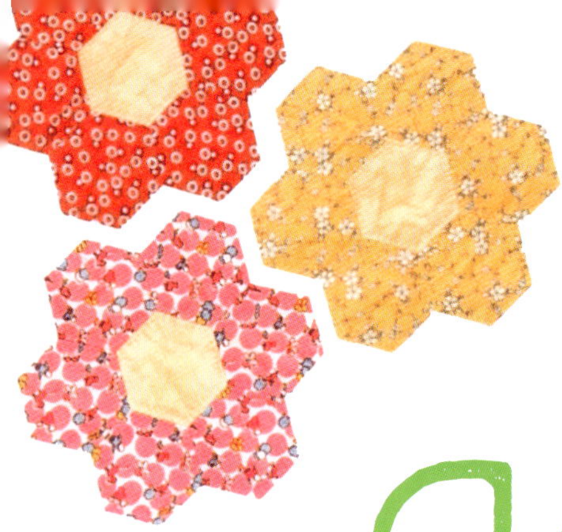

Hexagons Quilt

Finished Quilt Size: 96" x 92$^1/_2$" (244 cm x 235 cm)

Taffy-colored vintage fabric flowers combine with seven subtle stripes of tan and white to create this pretty English paper pieced quilt.

Shopping List

Yardage is based on 43"/44" (109 cm/112 cm) wide fabric with a usable width of 40" (102 cm). A fat eighth measures approximately 9" x 21" (23 cm x 53 cm.)

- ☐ 63 vintage print fat eighths for flower blocks
- ☐ $^3/_4$ yd (69 cm) of yellow print fabric for flower centers
- ☐ 6 yds (5.5 m) of white print fabric
- ☐ 4$^1/_2$ yds (4.1 m) of tan print fabric
- ☐ 3$^3/_4$ yds (3.4 m) of green print fabric for sashing
- ☐ 8$^1/_2$ yds (7.8 m) of fabric for backing
- ☐ 1 yd (91 cm) of small red check fabric for bias binding
- ☐ 104" x 101" (264 cm x 257 cm) piece of batting
- ☐ 1$^1/_2$" (38 mm) hexagon precut paper pieces (We used 1569.)
- ☐ 1$^1/_2$" (38 mm) half hexagon precut paper pieces (We used 44.)

TILIA

CUTTING THE PIECES

*Follow **Rotary Cutting**, page 42, and **Speed Cutting Fabric Shapes**, page 43, to cut fabric. For yardage, cut all strips from the selvage-to-selvage width of the fabric unless otherwise stated. For fat eighths, cut strips parallel to the long edge.*

From *each* fat eighth:

- For one flower block, cut 2 strips $3^1/_2$" wide. Cut 6 **hexagons**.

From yellow print fabric:

- Cut 7 strips $3^1/_2$" wide. Cut a total of 63 hexagons.

From white print fabric:

- Cut 56 strips $3^1/_2$" wide. Cut a total of 480 hexagons and 16 half hexagons.

From tan print fabric:

- Cut 42 strips $3^1/_2$" wide. Cut a total of 360 hexagons and 12 half hexagons.

From green print fabric:

- Cut 34 strips $3^1/_2$" wide. Cut a total of 288 hexagons and 16 half hexagons.

From small red check fabric:

- Cut a 32" square of fabric. Refer to **Making Continuous Bias Binding**, page 52, to make approximately 400" of $2^1/_4$" wide **bias binding**.

MAKING THE HEXAGONS

*Follow **English Paper Piecing**, page 43, to make quilt top.*

Make the following number of basted $1^1/_2$" hexagons and half hexagons:

- 63 sets of 6 matching vintage print full hexagons for flower blocks.
- 63 yellow print full hexagons for flower centers.
- 480 white full hexagons and 16 half hexagons.
- 360 tan full hexagons and 12 half hexagons.
- 288 green print full hexagons and 16 half hexagons for sashing.

MAKING THE BLOCKS

Vintage print flower blocks are surrounded with white or tan hexagons and then joined into 7 vertical rows of 9 flower blocks. The vertical rows alternate with green hexagon sashing strips.

Flower Block

1. Whipstitch, page 45, 1 yellow print center hexagon and 6 matching vintage print hexagons together **(Fig. 1)** to make a flower block. Make 63 flower blocks.

Fig. 1

Block 1

1. Whipstitch 12 white hexagons around one flower block (**Fig. 2**).

Fig. 2

2. Whipstitch 1 white hexagon to each of the 4 corners (**Fig. 3**).

Fig. 3

3. Whipstitch 2 white half hexagons to the top edge only to make **Block 1**.

Block 1

4. Repeat Steps 1-3 to make a total of 4 white and 3 tan Block 1's.

Block 2

1. Whipstitch 11 white hexagons around 1 flower block (**Fig. 4**). Do not whipstitch a hexagon to the top flower hexagon; this is where it will join Block 1.

Fig. 4

2. Whipstitch 1 white hexagon to each bottom corner to make **Block 2**.

Block 2

3. Repeat Steps 1-2 to make a total of 32 white and 24 tan Block 2's.

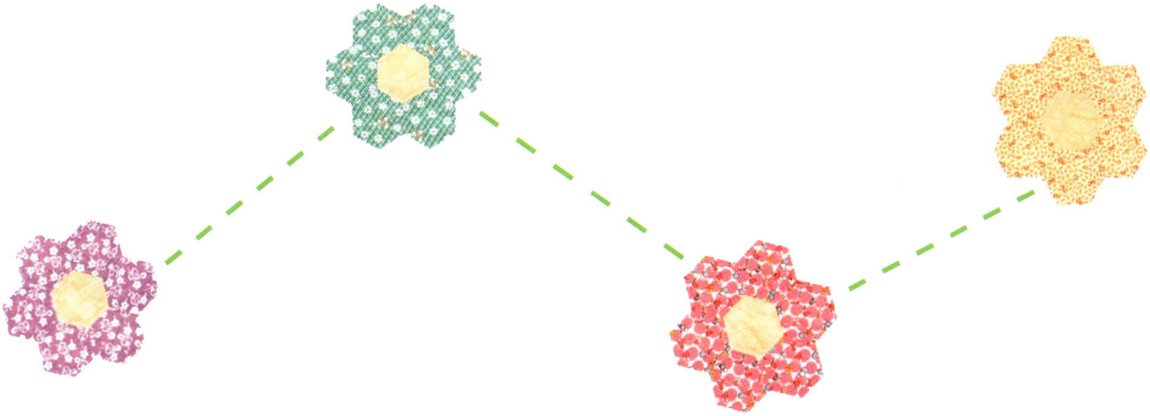

Quilt Top

Vertical Row 1

1. Whipstitch bottom edge of Block 1 to top edge of Block 2 **(Fig. 5)**.

Fig. 5

2. Continue whipstitching Block 2's together until there are a total of 8 Block 2's added to Block 1.
3. Whipstitch 2 white half hexagons to the bottom edge to make a straight bottom edge **(Fig. 6)**.

Fig. 6

4. Repeat Steps 1-3 to make a total of 4 white vertical Row 1's.

Vertical Row 2

1. Repeat Vertical Row 1, using tan Block 1's and tan hexagons and half hexagons to make Vertical Row 2.
2. Repeat to make a total of 3 tan vertical Row 2's.

Sashing

1. Whipstitch 36 green print hexagons end to end.
2. Whipstitch 1 half hexagon to each end **(Fig. 7)**.

Fig. 7

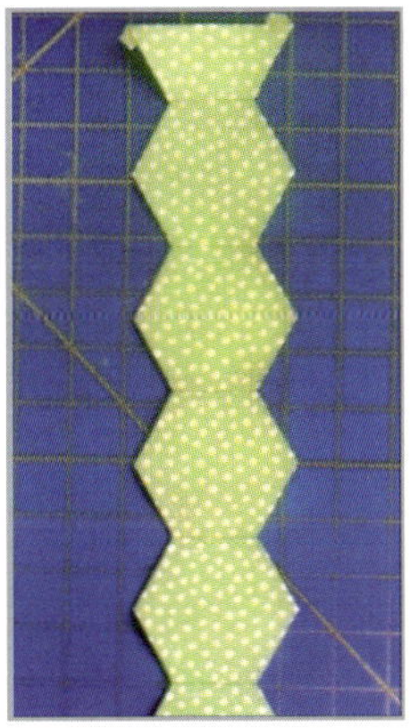

3. Repeat Steps 1-2 to make a total of 8 sashings.

ASSEMBLING THE QUILT TOP

*Refer to **Quilt Top** for assembly.*

1. Alternating colors and adding sashing in between, whipstitch 4 Vertical Row 1's, 3 Vertical Row 2's, and 6 sashings together.
2. Whipstitch 1 sashing to left hand side and 1 sashing to right hand side of quilt top.

COMPLETING THE QUILT

1. Remove all paper pieces. Press quilt top; do not unfold outside edges.
2. Follow **Quilting**, page 49, to mark, layer, and quilt as desired. Quilt shown is hand quilted $^1/_8$" from edge of each hexagon.
3. After quilting, trim points from sashings on quilt sides.
4. Follow **Attaching Binding with Mitered Corners**, page 53, to bind quilt.

Hexagons Pillow Sham

Finished Quilt Size: 25" x 23¹/₂" (64 cm x 60 cm)

The shams are pieced in the same simple way as the quilt; hexagons are stitched end to end and then joined in vertical rows.

Shopping List

Yardage is based on 43"/44" (109 cm/112 cm) wide fabric with a usable width of 40" (102 cm). Yardage given is for making one sham.

- ☐ approximately 1³/₈ yds (1.3 m) **total** of scraps of vintage prints
- ☐ 1 yd (91 cm) of muslin for sham front backing
- ☐ 1 yd (91 cm) of yellow print fabric for sham back and flap
- ☐ ⁷/₈ yd (80 cm) of small red check fabric for ties and binding
- ☐ 30" x 30" (76 mm x 76 cm) piece of lightweight batting
- ☐ 1¹/₂" (38 mm) hexagon precut paper pieces (We used 105.)
- ☐ 1¹/₂" (38 mm) half hexagon precut paper pieces (We used 10.)
- ☐ 26" x 26" (66 cm x 66 cm) European pillow form

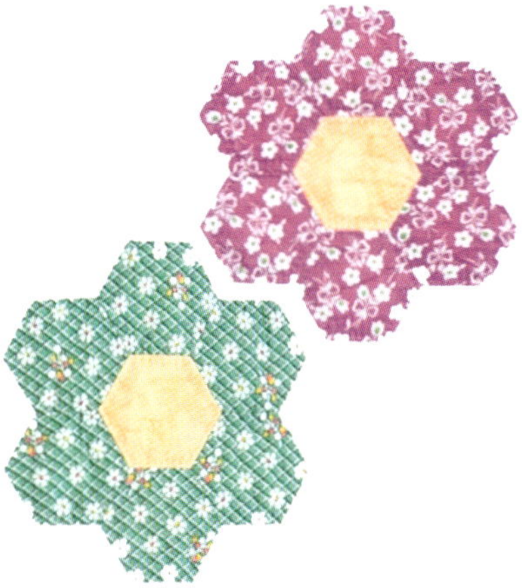

CUTTING THE PIECES

*Follow **Rotary Cutting**, page 42, and **Speed Cutting Fabric Shapes**, page 43, to cut fabric. Cut all strips from the selvage-to-selvage width of the fabric unless otherwise stated.*

From scraps of vintage prints:

- Cut 105 **hexagons** and 10 **half hexagons**.

From muslin:

- Cut **sham front backing** 30" x 30".

From yellow print fabric:

- Cut **sham back** 25" x $23^{1}/_{2}$".
- Cut **flap** $23^{1}/_{2}$" x 8".

From small red check fabric:

- Cut 3 strips $2^{1}/_{4}$" wide. From these strips, cut 6 **ties** $2^{1}/_{4}$" x 16".
- Cut an 20" x 20" square. Refer to **Making Continuous Bias Binding**, page 52, to make 140" of $2^{1}/_{4}$" wide **bias binding**.

MAKING THE HEXAGONS

*Follow **English Paper Piecing**, page 43, to make the sham.*

Make the following number of basted $1^{1}/_{2}$" hexagons and half hexagons:

- 105 full hexagons and 10 half hexagons from assorted vintage prints

MAKING THE SHAM FRONT

Hexagons and half hexagons are whipstitched together into rows and then the rows are whipstitched together to make the pillow sham front.

1. Whipstitch, page 45, 10 hexagons together end to end to make **Row 1**. Make 6 Row 1's.
2. Whipstitch 9 hexagons together end to end and add a half hexagon to each end to make **Row 2**. Make 5 Row 2's.
3. Alternating rows, join Row 1's and Row 2's together along the length **(Fig. 1)**.

Fig. 1

4. Remove all paper pieces. Press sham front; do not unfold outside edges.
5. Follow **Quilting**, page 49, to mark, layer, and quilt as desired using batting and **sham front backing** **(Fig. 2)**. Sham shown is hand quilted $^{1}/_{8}$" from edge of each hexagon.

Fig. 2

6. Trimming equally from each side, trim quilted sham front to 25" x 23 1/2".

MAKING AND ATTACHING THE TIES

1. Matching right sides, fold one **tie** in half lengthwise. Trim one end at a 45° angle. Stitch the long side and the angled end. Turn right side out and press. Repeat with the remaining ties.
2. Matching right sides and raw edges, position one tie at midpoint and one tie 2 1/2" from each corner on one edge of sham front that has half hexagons. Stitch in place using a scant 1/4" seam allowance.

FINISHING THE SHAM

1. Refer to **Attaching Binding with Mitered Corners**, page 53, bind the edge of the sham front with ties using **bias binding**.
2. Press 1 long edge of **flap** 1" to wrong side; press 1" to wrong side again. Stitch close to edge.
3. Matching wrong sides and raw edges, baste flap on one short end of **sham back** using a scant 1/4" seam allowance on three sides (Do not stitch along hemmed edge.)
4. Lay sham back on quilted sham front and mark position of 3 ties on right side of sham back.
5. Baste 3 ties in place on right side of sham back using a scant 1/4" seam allowance.
6. Bind edge of the sham back with ties using bias binding. Tie a knot in the end of each tie.
7. Matching wrong sides and raw edges, layer sham top and sham back (with flap in between). Baste through all layers around raw edges using a scant 1/4" seam allowance.
8. Press one raw end of bias binding 1/4" to wrong side. Beginning with pressed end, use bias binding to bind raw edges of sham, mitering corners and turning end 1/4" to wrong side. Whipstitch ends of binding closed.
9. Insert pillow form and tie to close.

Pajama Bag

Finished Size: 14" x 15" (36 cm x 38 cm)

Shopping List

Yardage is based on 43"/44" (109 cm/112 cm) wide fabric with a usable width of 40" (102 cm). Decorator-weight fabric may be 54" (137 cm) wide but the same yardage is required.

- ☐ approximately 3/4 yd (69 cm) **total** of assorted scraps of vintage print fabrics
- ☐ 5/8 yd (57 cm) of stripe decorator-weight fabric for top panels, top panel linings, and handles
- ☐ 1/2 yd (46 cm) of yellow print fabric for lining
- ☐ 5/8 yd (57 cm) of small red check fabric for bias binding
- ☐ 1/8 yd (11 cm) of purple polka dot fabric for handle lining
- ☐ 1/8 yd (11 cm) of red print fabric for letters
- ☐ 5/8 yd (57 cm) of muslin for backing
- ☐ 1/4 yd (23 cm) of 20" (51 cm) wide medium-weight fusible interfacing for lining reinforcement
- ☐ 38" x 20" (97 cm x 51 cm) piece of lightweight batting
- ☐ 1 1/2" (38 mm) hexagon precut paper pieces (We used 50.)
- ☐ 1 1/2" (38 mm) half hexagon precut paper pieces (We used 8.)
- ☐ paper-backed fusible web
- ☐ embroidery floss - black and assorted colors
- ☐ 7/8 yd (80 cm) of 1/2" (13 mm) wide (medium) lilac rickrack
- ☐ 10 assorted flower-shaped buttons
- ☐ 7/16" (11 mm) diameter red button
- ☐ four 1/2" (13 mm) leaf-shaped beads
- ☐ 14 pearl seed beads

Pajamas

CUTTING THE PIECES

Follow ***Rotary Cutting****, page 42, and* ***Speed Cutting Fabric Shapes****, page 43, to cut fabric. For yardage, cut all strips from the selvage-to-selvage width of the fabric unless otherwise stated.*

From scraps of vintage prints:

- 50 **hexagons** and 8 **half hexagons.**

From stripe decorator-weight fabric:

- Cut 2 **top panels** 6 1/4" x 15" with stripes running parallel to the long edge.
- Cut 2 **top panel linings** 3" x 15" with stripes running parallel to the long edge.
- Cut 2 **handles** 1 1/2" x 17" with stripes running parallel to the long edge.

From yellow print fabric:

- Cut **lining** 30" x 15" .

From small red check fabric:

- Cut a 20" x 20" square. Refer to **Making Continuous Bias Binding**, page 52, to make 140" of 2 1/4" wide **bias binding**.

From purple polka dot fabric:

- Cut 2 **handle linings** 2 1/2" x 18".

From muslin:

- Cut **backing** 32" x 17".

From interfacing:

- Cut 2 **top panel linings** 2 1/2" x 15".

From batting:

- Cut **outer bag** 31" x 16" .
- Cut 2 **handles** 2 1/2" x 18".

PREPARING FUSIBLE APPLIQUÉS

Appliqué patterns, page 37, do not include seam allowances. Follow ***Preparing Fusible Appliqués****, page 49, to cut out appliqués.*

From red print fabric:

- Cut **letters** to spell "Pajamas."

MAKING THE HEXAGONS

Follow ***English Paper Piecing****, page 43, to make the bag.*

Make the following number of basted 1 1/2" hexagons and half hexagons:

- 50 full hexagons and 8 half hexagons from assorted vintage prints

MAKING THE OUTER BAG

Hexagons and half hexagons are whipstitched together into rows and then the rows are whipstitched together to make the outer bag. Use a 1/2" seam allowance unless otherwise indicated.

1. Whipstitch, page 45, 6 **hexagons** together to make **Row 1**. Make 5 Row 1's.
2. Whipstitch 5 hexagons and 2 **half hexagons** together to make **Row 2**. Make 4 Row 2's.
3. Alternating rows, join Row 1's and Row 2's together.
4. Remove all paper pieces. Press outer bag; do not unfold outside edges. Using a rotary cutter and ruler, trim off points of hexagons on each short side so that piece measures 19 1/2" x 15".
5. Matching right sides, sew one long edge of one **top panel** to each short edge of pieced panel. Press seam allowances open.
6. Fuse **letters** to top panel. Use 2 strands of black embroidery floss to work a Buttonhole Stitch, page 55, around the letters.

QUILTING AND EMBELLISHING THE OUTER BAG

1. Layer the batting on top of the **backing**. Place the outer bag right side up on top of the batting.
2. Hand quilt 1/4" from outside edge of each hexagon.
3. For quilting on top panel, use 1 strand of embroidery floss and a Running Stitch, page 55, to stitch a rectangle through all layers around the word "pajamas." Use 1 strand of embroidery floss and a Running Stitch to stitch along the stripes in the fabric using various colors as desired.
4. Trim backing and batting even with outer bag.

5. Use embroidery floss and a Running Stitch to sew a piece of rickrack over each seam.
6. Sew on flower buttons, leaf beads, and pearl seed beads as desired. Sew on the red button for the dot over the letter "j."
7. Matching right sides and short edges of outer bag, fold bag in half; stitch side seams. Clip corners and press seam allowances open; turn right sides out.

MAKING THE LINING

1. Fuse 1 piece of interfacing **top panel lining** to wrong side along 1 long edge of each fabric **top panel lining**. Press non-interfaced edge of top panel lining 1/2" to wrong side.
2. Matching wrong side of top panel lining to right side of **lining**, machine baste one top panel lining to each short end of lining. Machine stitch close to bottom folded edge of top panel lining.
3. On the top panel linings, use 1 strand of embroidery floss and a Running Stitch to stitch along the stripes in the fabric using various colors as desired.
4. Matching right sides and short edges, fold lining in half; stitch side seams. Clip corners and press seams open; do not turn lining right side out.
5. Matching wrong sides, slip lining inside the outer bag. Machine baste through all layers a scant 1/4" from the top edge.
6. Refer to **Attaching Binding with Mitered Corners**, page 53, to sew binding to top edge of bag.

MAKING AND ADDING THE HANDLES

1. Place 1 **handle lining**, right side down, on work surface. Place 1 batting **handle** on handle lining. Center 1 **handle**, right side up, on batting.
2. Using 1 strand of floss, work Running Stitches through all layers in rows along the stripes on the handle.
3. Trim backing and batting even with handle edges.
4. Mitering corners, attach binding to edges of handle **(Fig. 1)**.

Fig. 1

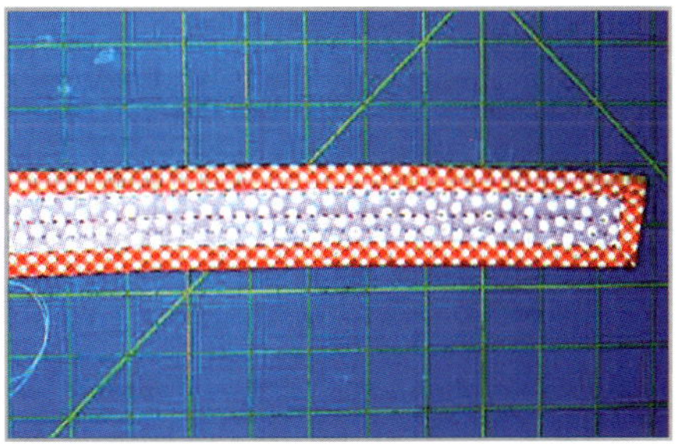

5. Measure 4" from each short end of handle; mark with a pin. Fold the handle in half between the pins **(Fig. 2)**. Whipstitch the bound edges together between the pins.

Fig. 2

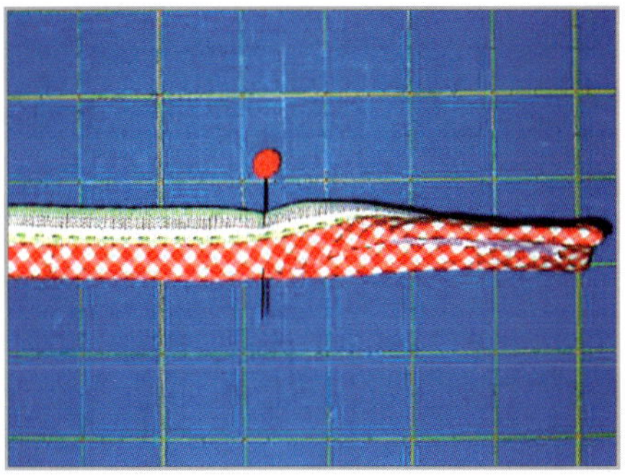

6. Repeat Steps 1-5 to make the remaining handle.
7. For one handle end, pin the outside edge 3" from the side seam of the bag and the bottom edge 1 1/2" from the top edge of the bag. Machine stitch a square and "X" to attach handle. Pin the remaining handle end 3" from the opposite side seam of the bag and the bottom edge 1 1/2" from the top edge of the bag. Secure in the same manner. Repeat for the remaining handle on the opposite side of the bag.

Trellis Quilt

Finished Quilt Size: 89" x 89" (226 cm x 226 cm)
Finished Block Size: 7" x 7" (18 cm x 18 cm)

Inspired by a garden trellis, this fun queen-sized quilt has hand appliquéd vintage flowers and a cotton candy-striped border.

Shopping List

Yardage is based on 43"/44" (109 cm/112 cm) wide fabric with a usable width of 40" (102 cm).

- ☐ $2^3/_8$ yds (2.2 m) of white print fabric for appliquéd flower backgrounds
- ☐ $2^3/_8$ yds (2.2 m) of pink print fabric for setting squares and triangles
- ☐ $2^3/_4$ yds (2.5 m) of dark pink print fabric for sashing and ribbon appliqués
- ☐ $2^3/_4$ yds (2.5 m) of pink ticking stripe fabric for borders
- ☐ 1 yd (91 cm) of small red check fabric for bias binding
- ☐ 44 squares $6^1/_2$" x $6^1/_2$" (17 cm 17 cm) of assorted small and medium scale print fabrics for large flower appliqués
- ☐ scraps of assorted small and medium scale print fabrics for medium and small flower appliqués
- ☐ scraps of green assorted small scale print fabrics for leaf appliqués
- ☐ $^3/_8$ yd (34 cm) of small yellow check fabric for flower center appliqués
- ☐ paper-backed fusible web
- ☐ black embroidery floss
- ☐ 97" x 97" (246 cm x 246 cm) piece of batting
- ☐ $8^1/_8$ yds (7.4 m) of fabric for backing

CUTTING THE PIECES

*Follow **Rotary Cutting**, page 42, to cut fabric. Cut all strips from the selvage-to-selvage width of the fabric unless otherwise stated. White background squares and pink print setting triangles are cut slightly larger and will be trimmed after stitching. Borders are cut longer than needed and will be trimmed to fit quilt top center. All measurements include 1/4" seam allowances.*

From white print fabric:

- Cut 9 strips 8 1/2" wide. From these strips, cut 36 **background squares** 8 1/2" x 8 1/2".

From pink print fabric:

- Cut 5 strips 7 1/2" wide. From these strips, cut 25 **setting squares** 7 1/2" x 7 1/2".
- Cut 2 strips 11 1/2" wide. From these strips, cut 5 squares 11 1/2" x 11 1/2". Cut each square in half twice diagonally to make 20 **large setting triangles**.
- Cut 2 squares 7 1/4" x 7 1/4". Cut each square in half diagonally to make 4 **small setting triangles**.

From dark pink print fabric:

- Cut 20 strips 1 1/2" wide. Sew these strips together to make one long strip. From this strip, cut 8 **narrow borders** 1 1/2" x 94".
- Cut 15 strips 1 1/2" wide. From these strips, cut 72 **short sashing strips** 1 1/2" x 7 1/2".
- Cut 2 strips 1 1/2" wide. From ***each*** strip, cut 1 **sashing strip** 1 1/2" x 9 1/2" and 1 **sashing strip** 1 1/2" x 25 1/2".
- Cut 3 strips 1 1/2" wide. Sew these strips together to make one long strip. From this strip, cut 2 **sashing strips** 1 1/2" x 41 1/2".
- Cut 3 strips 1 1/2" wide. Sew these strips together to make one long strip. From this strip, cut 2 **sashing strips** 1 1/2" x 57 1/2".
- Cut 4 strips 1 1/2" wide. Sew these strips together to make one long strip. From this strip, cut 2 **sashing strips** 1 1/2" x 73 1/2".
- Cut 5 strips 1 1/2" wide. Sew these strips together to make one long strip. From this strip, cut 2 **sashing strips** 1 1/2" x 89 1/2".

From pink ticking stripe fabric:

- Cut 4 *lengthwise* **middle borders** 8 1/2" x 94 ".

From small red check fabric:

- Cut a square 32" x 32". Refer to **Making Continuous Bias Binding**, page 52, to make approximately 380" of 2 1/4" wide **bias binding**.

CUTTING THE APPLIQUÉS

*Refer to **Preparing Fusible Appliqués**, page 49, to make appliqués from patterns, pages 40-41. Appliqué patterns are printed in reverse and do not include seam allowances.*

From dark pink print fabric:

- Cut 8 **ribbons**; cut 8 ribbons in reverse.
- Cut 8 **ribbon ends**; cut 8 ribbon ends in reverse.

From small or medium scale print squares:

- Cut 44 **large flowers**.

From small or medium scale print fabrics:

- Cut 16 **medium flowers**.
- Cut 16 **small flowers**.

From scraps of assorted green small scale print fabrics:

- Cut a *total* of approximately 92 small and large **leaves**.

From small yellow check fabric:

- Cut 44 **large flower centers**.
- Cut 16 **medium flower centers**.
- Cut 16 **small flower centers**.

MAKING THE APPLIQUÉ BLOCKS

Flower Block

1. Fold a white **background square** into quarters and lightly press to mark center of square.
2. Aligning flower petals with pressed lines on background fabric, fuse 1 **large flower** to each background square. Fuse **large flower center** to each flower.
3. Using two strands of black embroidery floss, work Buttonhole Stitch, page 55, around the flowers and flower centers.
4. Press completed block. Centering flower, trim block to 7 1/2" x 7 1/2". Repeat to make a total of 36 flower blocks.

ASSEMBLING THE QUILT TOP CENTER

*Follow **Machine Piecing and Sewing**, page 46, and **Pressing**, page 47, to complete quilt. Refer to **Assembly Diagram** to assemble quilt top center.*

1. Aligning 1 edge, stitch flower blocks, **setting squares**, **short sashing strips**, and **large setting triangles** together in diagonal rows. Press seam allowances toward the sashing strips. On opposite edge, trim points of triangles even with sashing strips.
2. Alternating rows with sashing strips, stitch the diagonal rows together.
3. Centering the triangle on the sashing strip, stitch a **small setting triangle** to each corner. Press the seam allowances toward the sashing strips.
4. Trim the quilt top center to 68$^{3}/_{8}$" x 68$^{3}/_{8}$".

MAKING AND ADDING THE BORDERS

*Refer to **Quilt Top** for assembly.*

1. Sew 1 **narrow border** to each long edge of 1 **middle border**. Press seam allowances open. Repeat to make a total of 4 borders.
2. Refer to **Adding Mitered Borders**, page 47, to add borders.

APPLIQUÉING THE BORDERS

1. To mark center of borders for appliqué, fold quilt top in half and lightly press each border. Centering appliqués, fuse appliqués to border top, bottom, sides, and corners.
2. Using two strands of black embroidery floss, work Buttonhole Stitch around the appliqués.

Assembly Diagram

FINISHING THE QUILT

1. Follow **Quilting**, page 49, to mark, layer, and quilt as desired. Our quilt was stitched with a flower design in each setting square, in the ditch around each appliqué, a meandering vine design in each sashing and narrow border, and a meandering flower design in the middle border.
2. Follow **Attaching Binding with Mitered Corners**, page 53, to bind quilt using **bias binding**.

Quilt Top

Floral Appliqué Pillow

Finished Size: 29" x 19" (74 cm x 48 cm)

Shopping List

Yardage is based on 43"/44" (109 cm/112 cm) wide fabric with a usable width of 40" (102 cm). Yardage given is for making 1 pillow.

- ☐ $^5/_8$ yd (57 cm) of pink ticking stripe fabric for appliqué background
- ☐ $^3/_8$ yd (34 cm) of dark pink print fabric for borders and appliqué
- ☐ $^5/_8$ yd (57 cm) of pink floral print fabric for back of pillow
- ☐ $2^1/_2$ yds (2.3 m) of muslin for lining
- ☐ $^5/_8$ yd (57 cm) of small red check fabric for binding
- ☐ scraps of small and medium scale prints for flower appliqués
- ☐ scraps of green small scale prints for leaf appliqués
- ☐ 47" x 49" (119 cm x 124 cm) piece of lightweight batting
- ☐ black embroidery floss
- ☐ three $^{15}/_{16}$" (24 mm) diameter buttons
- ☐ paper-backed fusible web
- ☐ $^3/_8$ yd (34 cm) of $^1/_2$" (13 mm) wide white cotton twill tape (button loops)
- ☐ 26" x 16" (66 cm x 41 cm) pillow form

CUTTING THE PIECES

*Follow **Rotary Cutting**, page 42, to cut fabric. All measurements include 1/2" seam allowances.*

From pink ticking stripe:

- Cut one **appliqué background** 28" x 18".

From dark pink print fabric:

- Cut two **long borders** 1 1/2" x 32".
- Cut two **short borders** 1 1/2" x 22".

From pink floral print fabric:

- Cut **pillow back** 41" x 20".

From muslin:

- Cut **front lining** 34" x 24".
- Cut **back lining** 46" x 25".

From small red check fabric:

- Cut a 20" x 20" square. Refer to **Making Continuous Bias Binding**, page 52, to make 150" of 2 1/4" wide **bias binding**.

From batting:

- Cut **front batting** 33" x 23".
- Cut **back batting** 45" x 24".

CUTTING THE APPLIQUÉS

*Follow **Preparing Fusible Appliqués**, page 49, to use appliqués. Appliqué patterns, pages 40-41, are printed in reverse and do not include seam allowances.*

From dark pink print fabric:

- Cut 1 **large flower**.

From small or medium scale print fabric:

- Cut 4 **medium flowers**.
- Cut 6 **small flowers**.

From scraps of assorted green small scale print fabrics:

- Cut 7 **large leaves**.
- Cut 20 **small leaves**.

From small yellow check fabric:

- Cut 1 **large flower center**.
- Cut 4 **medium flower centers**.
- Cut 6 **small flower centers**.

MAKING THE PILLOW FRONT

Use a 1/4" seam allowance throughout.

1. Arrange and fuse appliqués to **appliqué background**.
2. Using two strands of black embroidery floss, work Buttonhole Stitch, page 55, around the appliqués.
3. Keeping the appliqué design centered, trim the appliqué background to 27" x 17".
4. Refer to **Adding Mitered Borders**, page 47, to add borders to appliqué background to make pillow front.
5. Layer the appliquéd pillow front (right side up), **front batting**, and **front lining**. Quilt as desired. Our pillow front is outline quilted around the group of flowers, with a meandering floral vine across the background, and meandering quilting in each border. After quilting, trim the batting and lining even with the pillow front square.

MAKING THE PILLOW BACK

1. Layer **pillow back** (right side up), **back batting**, and **back lining**. Quilt as desired. Our pillow back is quilted with a meandering floral vine. After quilting, trim the quilted back into two pillow backs measuring $19\frac{1}{2}$" x 18".
2. Mark the center of one long edge of one pillow back with a pin.
3. To make button loops, fold $\frac{1}{2}$" wide twill tape in half lengthwise; stitch. Cut into three 3" lengths. Matching raw ends, fold one length in half; pin to marked center of one pillow back. Measure 5" on either side of the first loop and pin a folded length at each mark. Stitch in place a scant $\frac{1}{4}$" from raw edge.
4. Refer to **Attaching Binding with Mitered Corners**, page 53, to bind one long edge of each pillow back, over raw edges of twill tape. Bind one long edge of the remaining pillow back.
5. Matching lining sides and overlapping bound edges, pin the pillow backs to the pillow front. Sew 1 button on the pillow back at each loop (**Fig. 1**).

Fig. 1

FINISHING THE PILLOW

1. Taking a scant $\frac{1}{4}$" seam allowance, stitch through all layers around the outside edges.
2. To make the flange, stitch in the ditch between the border and the appliqué background.
3. Bind the raw edges. Insert the pillow form.

Laundry Bag

Finished Size: 16" x 26" (41 cm x 66 cm)

Shopping List

Yardage is based on 43"/44" (109 cm/112 cm) wide fabric with a usable width of 40" (102 cm). Decorator-weight fabric and linen may be 54" (137 cm) wide but the same yardage is required.

- ☐ 5/8 yd (57 cm) of stripe decorator-weight fabric for bottom and middle panel
- ☐ 1/2 yd (46 cm) of white linen fabric for top
- ☐ 1 5/8 yds (1.5 m) of yellow print fabric for lining
- ☐ 3/8 yd (34 cm) of purple polka dot fabric for binding
- ☐ 1/8 yd (11 cm) of red print fabric for letter appliqués
- ☐ scraps of lilac, yellow, red, orange, and pink small print fabrics for flower appliqués
- ☐ scraps of green print fabric for leaf appliqués
- ☐ paper-backed fusible web
- ☐ 2 1/8 yds (1.9 m) of 1/2" (13 mm) wide (medium) pink rickrack
- ☐ 2 3/8 yds (2.2 m) of 1/2" (13 mm) wide white twill tape for drawstring
- ☐ embroidery floss - lilac, green, yellow, red, orange, pink, and black
- ☐ assorted buttons for flower centers (We used 17.)
- ☐ pearl seed beads (We used 16.)
- ☐ water- or air-soluble fabric marking pen

Laundry

CUTTING THE PIECES

*Follow **Rotary Cutting**, page 42, to cut fabric. All measurements include 1/2" seam allowances.*

From stripe decorator-weight fabric:

- Cut 2 **middle panels** 7" x 17" with stripes running parallel to the longest side.
- Cut **bottom** 17" x 13 1/2" with stripes running parallel to the shortest side.

From white linen fabric:

- Cut 2 **tops** 17" x 14 1/4" .

From yellow print fabric:

- Cut **lining** 17" x 52".

From purple polka dot fabric:

- Cut a square 12" x 12". Refer to **Making Continuous Bias Binding**, page 52, to make approximately 40" of 2 1/4" wide **bias binding**.

PREPARING FUSIBLE APPLIQUÉS

*Follow **Preparing Fusible Appliqués**, page 49, to use appliqués. Appliqué patterns, page 38, are printed in reverse and do not include seam allowances.*

From red print fabric:

- Cut desired number of **leaves**. (We used 43.)

From scraps of small print fabrics:

- Cut **letters** to spell "Laundry."

From scraps of green print fabric:

- Cut desired number of **flowers**. (We used 17.)

MAKING THE BOTTOM

Match right sides and raw edges and use a 1/2" seam allowance throughout. Press seam allowances open.

1. Using 1 strand of floss, work Running Stitches, page 55, in assorted colors of floss as desired on **bottom**, using stripes in fabric as a guide.
2. Reserving some flower and leaf appliqués for middle panel, arrange **flowers** and **leaves** on bottom as desired. Using 2 strands of embroidery floss, work a Buttonhole Stitch, page 55, around the flowers. Using 2 strands of green floss, work a Buttonhole Stitch around the leaves.
3. Sew a button to the center of each flower.

MAKING THE MIDDLE PANEL

1. Using 1 strand of floss, work Running Stitches in assorted colors of floss on 1 **middle panel**, using stripes in fabric as a guide; set aside.
2. Arrange **letters** on remaining middle panel as desired; fuse. Using 2 strands of black floss, work a Buttonhole Stitch around the letters.
3. Using 1 strand of floss, work Running Stitches in a rectangle around the letters. Using 1 strand of floss, work Running Stitches in assorted colors of floss on panel, using stripes in fabric as a guide.
4. Arrange the remaining flowers and leaves around letters as desired; fuse. Using 2 strands of embroidery floss, work a Buttonhole Stitch around the flowers. Using 2 strands of green floss, work Buttonhole Stitch around the leaves. Sew a button to the center of each flower. Sew seed beads around each flower as desired.

MAKING THE TOP

1. Leaving approximately 4" along one long edge of **top** empty, use pen to trace embroidery flowers and leaves as desired onto each top.
2. Using 2 strands of embroidery floss, work an Outline Stitch, page 55, in assorted colors as desired for flowers, yellow floss for flower centers, and green floss for leaves.

MAKING THE BAG

1. Matching long raw edges, sew the middle panels to the bottom.
2. Matching long raw edges, sew 1 top to each middle panel.
3. On right side, center rickrack over each seam and sew in place (**Fig. 1**).

Fig. 1

4. Matching right sides and short edges, fold bag in half. On each side, measure down 2" from top edge; mark with a pin. Measure down 3" from the top edge and mark with another pin (**Fig. 2**).

Fig. 2

5. Backstitching when starting and stopping, stitch side seams together, leaving the seam open between the pins. Turn bag right side out (**Fig. 3**).

Fig. 3

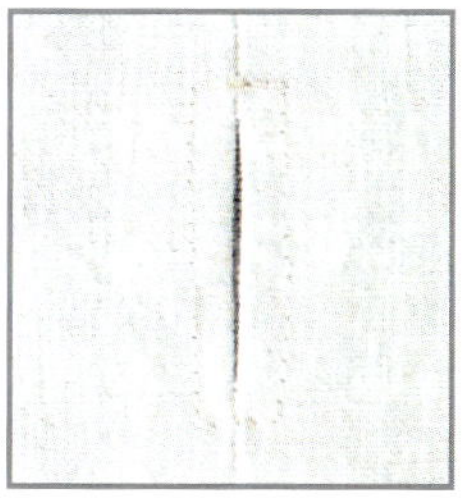

6. Matching right side and short edges, fold **lining** in half. Stitch side seams together; press seam allowances open.
7. Matching wrong sides, top edge, and side seams, place lining in bag. Machine baste top edges together using a scant $^{1}/_{4}$" seam allowance.
8. Refer to **Attaching Binding with Mitered Corners**, page 53, to sew binding to top edge.
9. For casing for drawstring, measure and mark stitching lines parallel to top edge at top and bottom of side seam openings (**Fig. 4**); stitch in place.

Fig. 4

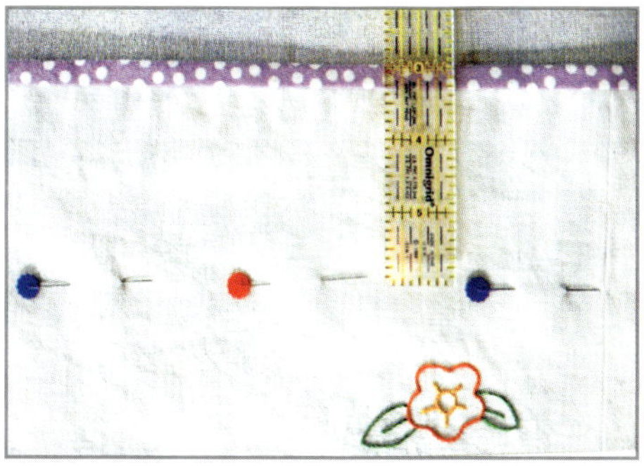

10. Cut two 42" lengths of twill tape. Press 1 end $^{1}/_{4}$" to wrong side. Press $^{1}/_{4}$" to wrong side again; stitch in place. Repeat for remaining ends.
11. Using a safety pin, thread 1 length of tape through 1 opening, all the way around the bag, and out through the same opening; knot the ends. Thread the remaining length of tape through the opposite opening, around the bag, and out through the same opening; knot the ends.

Floral-Edge Pillow Cover

Finished Size: 30" x 20" (76 cm x 51 cm)

Shopping List

Yardage is based on 54" (137 cm) wide linen fabric with a usable width of 50" (127 cm) and will make 1 pillow cover.

- ☐ 1 3/8 yds (1.3 m) of white linen fabric
- ☐ Scraps of lilac, yellow, red, orange, and pink small print fabrics for flower appliqués
- ☐ Scrap of green print fabric for leaf appliqués
- ☐ Scrap of yellow print fabric for flower center appliqués
- ☐ embroidery floss - lilac, green, yellow, red, orange, and pink
- ☐ 3 yds (2.7 m) of white pompom fringe trim
- ☐ paper-backed fusible web
- ☐ water- or air-soluble fabric marking pen
- ☐ 30" x 20" (76 cm x 51 cm) pillow form

CUTTING THE PIECES

*Follow **Rotary Cutting**, page 42, to cut fabric. All measurements include 1/2" seam allowances.*

From white linen:

- Cut one **pillow cover front** 38" x 21".
- Cut two **pillow cover backs** 19" x 21".

CUTTING THE APPLIQUÉS

*Refer to **Preparing Fusible Appliqués**, page 49, to make appliqués from patterns, page 38. Appliqué patterns are printed in reverse and do not include seam allowances.*

From scraps of small print fabrics:

- Cut desired number of **flowers**. (We used 11.)

From scraps of green small print fabrics:

- Cut desired number of **leaves**. (We used 29.)

From scraps of yellow print fabric:

- Cut desired number of **flower centers**. (We used 11.)

MAKING THE PILLOW COVER FRONT

Use a 1/2" seam allowance throughout.

1. To mark the hem, press one short edge of the **pillow cover front** to the wrong side 1" and then 6"; open.
2. Using the pen, trace desired number of flowers, flower centers and leaves that you would like to embroidery in an area approximately 5 1/2" wide above the second crease.
3. Using two strands of embroidery floss, work an Outline Stitch, page 55, in assorted colors as desired for flowers, yellow floss for flower centers, and green floss for leaves (**Fig. 1**).

Fig. 1

4. Fuse the appliqués in place among the embroidered flowers.
5. Using two strands of embroidery floss, work a Buttonhole Stitch, page 55, around the flowers. Using two strands of yellow floss, work a Buttonhole Stitch around the flower centers. Using two strands of green floss, work a Buttonhole Stitch around the leaves (**Fig. 2**).

Fig. 2

6. Refold the hem and stitch close to the folded edge **(Fig. 3)**.

Fig. 3

7. Matching raw edges, pin the trim on the right side of the pillow cover front, gently rounding the corners and overlapping the ends. Baste the trim in place 1/4" from the raw edge.

MAKING THE PILLOW COVER

1. To hem each **pillow cover back**, press one long edge to wrong side 1"; press 1" to wrong side again. Stitch in place close to the fold.
2. Matching right sides and overlapping the hemmed edges, pin pillow cover backs to pillow cover front with the trim sandwiched in between. Stitch around the outside edges **(Fig. 4)**.

Fig. 4

3. Trim the points off the corners to reduce bulk and turn the pillow cover right side out **(Fig. 5)**.

Fig. 5

4. Press the pillow cover and insert the pillow form.

Lavender Sachet

Finished Size: 5" x 6 3/4" (13 cm x 17 cm)

Shopping List

Supplies and instructions given are for making one appliquéd sachet. Omit the appliqués for a fast and easy gift.

- ☐ 5 1/2" x 17" (14 cm x 43 cm) piece of fabric for sachet
- ☐ scraps of small print fabrics for flowers (optional)
- ☐ scraps of green small print fabrics for leaves (optional)
- ☐ scrap of small yellow check fabric for flower centers (optional)
- ☐ black embroidery floss
- ☐ paper-backed fusible web (optional)
- ☐ 1 yd (91 cm) of 1/8" to 1/4" (3 mm to 6 mm) wide ribbon
- ☐ dried lavender

CUTTING THE APPLIQUÉS

Refer to ***Preparing Fusible Appliqués****, page 49, to make appliqués from patterns, page 39. Appliqué patterns are printed in reverse and do not include seam allowances.*

From small print fabrics:

- Cut 1 **large flower**.
- Cut 1 **medium flower**.
- Cut 1 **small flower**.

From green small print fabrics:

- Cut 5 **medium leaves**.
- Cut 2 **small leaves**.

From small yellow check fabrics:

- Cut 1 **large flower center**.
- Cut 1 **medium flower center**.
- Cut 1 **small flower center**.

MAKING THE BAG

Use a ¼" seam allowance throughout.

1. Matching wrong sides and short edges, fold fabric in half; press bottom edge.
2. Fuse flowers, leaves, and flower centers to bag above crease; unfold. Using two strands of black embroidery floss, work a Buttonhole Stitch, page 55, around the appliqués (**Fig. 1**).

Fig. 1

3. Matching right sides and short edges, fold fabric in half. Measure and mark with pins at 2½" and 3" from the top edge (**Fig. 2**). Sew the side seam, leaving stitching open between pins. Repeat on remaining side seam. Press seam allowances open. Stitch around each opening close to edge to reinforce.

Fig. 2

4. To make drawstring casing, press the top edge ¼" to wrong side. Press the folded edge 1½" to wrong side. Stitch close to folded edge and again ½" away (**Fig. 3**). Turn bag right side out; press.

Fig. 3

5. Cut ribbon into two 18" lengths. Using a safety pin, thread 1 length through 1 opening, all the way around the sachet, and out through the same opening; knot the ends. Thread the remaining length through the opposite opening, all the way around the sachet, and out through the same opening (**Fig. 4**). Knot and trim ends. Fill bag with lavender and pull ribbons to close.

Fig. 4

Patterns

Pajama Bag

Letters

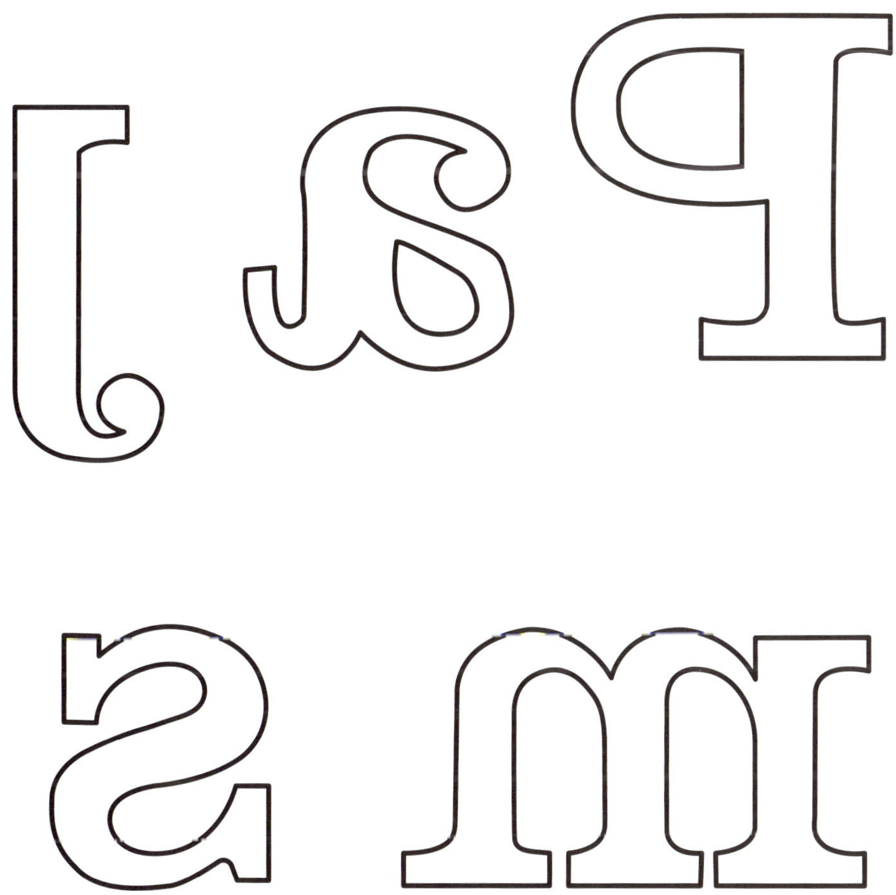

Laundry Bag

Floral Edge Pillow Cover and Laundry Bag

Large Embroidery Flowers

Flower and Leaf Appliques

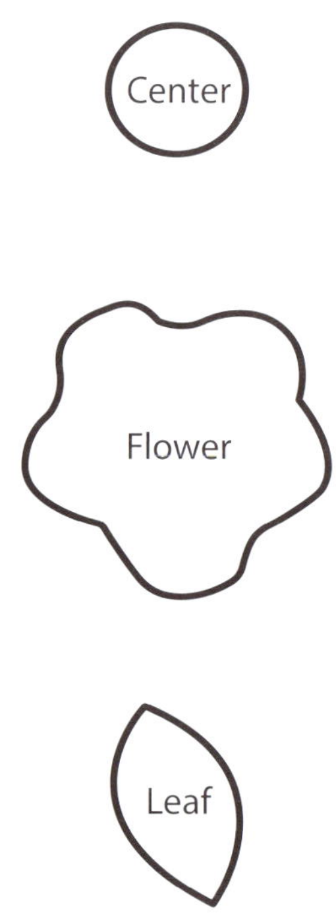

Lavender Sachet

Large Flower | Medium Flower | Small Flower

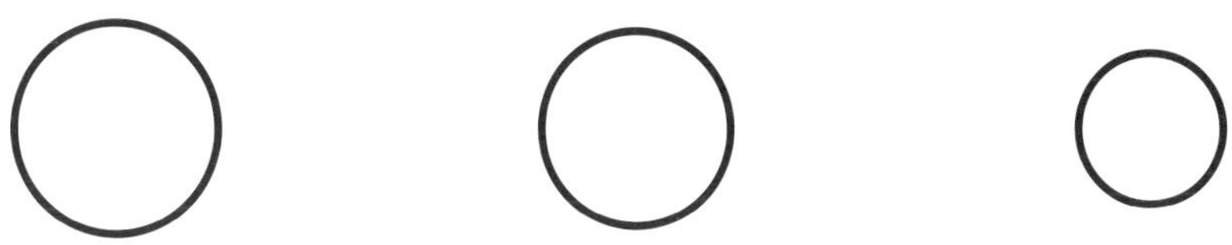

Large Flower Center | Medium Flower Center | Small Flower Center

Leaves

Medium

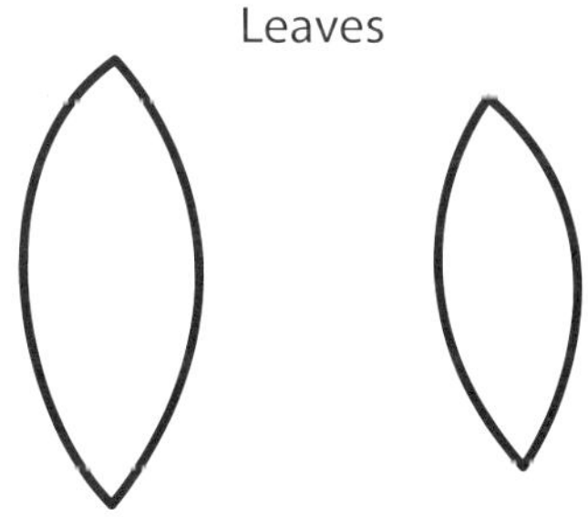

Small

Trellis Quilt and Pillow

Trellis Quilt and Pillow

Trellis Quilt

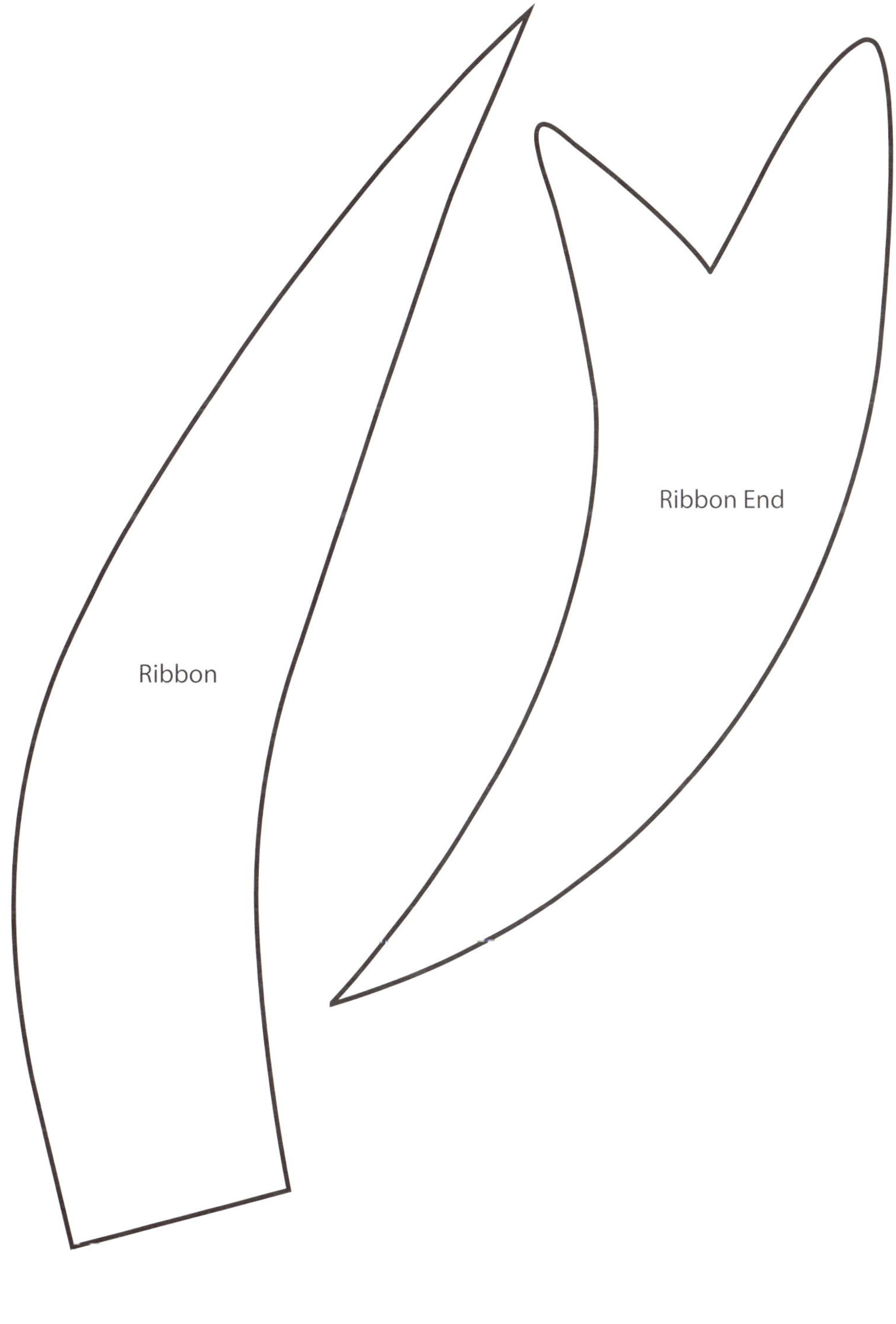

GENERAL INSTRUCTIONS

To make your project easier and more enjoyable, we encourage you to carefully read all of the general instructions, study the color photographs, and familiarize yourself with the individual project instructions before beginning.

FABRICS

SELECTING FABRICS

Choose high-quality, medium-weight 100% cotton and 100% linen (where instructed) fabrics. All-cotton fabrics hold a crease better, fray less, and are easier to quilt than cotton/polyester blends.

Yardage requirements listed for each project are based on 43"/44" wide cotton fabric with a "usable" width of 40" and 54" wide linen fabric with a "usable" width of 50" after shrinkage and trimming selvages. Actual usable width will probably vary slightly from fabric to fabric. Our recommended yardage lengths should be adequate for occasional re-squaring of fabric when many cuts are required.

PREPARING FABRICS

Machine wash fabrics (including linen) in warm water with a small amount of mild laundry detergent. Do not use fabric softener. Rinse well and then dry fabrics in the dryer, checking long fabric lengths occasionally to make sure they are not tangled. Remove fabrics from dryer while they are slightly damp. Refold each fabric lengthwise (as it was on the bolt) with wrong sides together and matching selvages.

Before cutting, prepare fabrics with a steam iron set on cotton or linen and starch or sizing. The starch or sizing will give the fabric a crisp finish. This will make cutting more accurate and may make piecing easier.

ROTARY CUTTING

CUTTING FROM YARDAGE

- Place fabric on work surface with fold closest to you.
- Cut all strips from the selvage-to-selvage width of the fabric unless otherwise indicated in project instructions.
- Square left edge of fabric using rotary cutter and rulers **(Figs. 1-2)**.

Fig. 1

Fig. 2

- To cut each strip required for a project, place ruler over cut edge of fabric, aligning desired marking on ruler with cut edge; make cut (**Fig. 3**).

Fig. 3

- When cutting several strips from a single piece of fabric, it is important to make sure that cuts remain at a perfect right angle to the fold; square fabric as needed.

CUTTING FROM FAT EIGHTHS

- If cutting strips parallel to the long edge, place fat eighth on work surface with short edge closest to you. Cut all strips parallel to the long edge of the fabric in the same manner as cutting from yardage.

- To cut each strip, place ruler over cut edge of fabric, aligning desired marking on ruler with cut edge; make cut.

ENGLISH PAPER PIECING

English paper piecing is an old-fashioned method for hand piecing quilt tops. Fabric shapes are folded over paper pieces and temporarily basted into place. The basted shapes are then held right sides together and whipstitched along the folded edges. The basting and the papers are then removed prior to quilting.

USING PRECUT PAPER SHAPES

Precut papers in all shapes and sizes are available at quilt shops and online. When buying precut shapes, the size given indicates the length of each side. The precut shapes are cut from sturdy paper and can be used two or three times. So save all your used papers to re-use in future projects.

SPEED CUTTING FABRIC SHAPES

Fabric shapes can be rotary cut quickly and easily. Just invest in a 1" x 6" ruler and a rotating cutting mat and you'll be stacking up fabric shapes in a matter of minutes!

Start with strips cut from the width of the fabric. This method allows for very little waste of fabric. The project instructions will tell you the width to cut the strips.

The typical 1/4" seam allowance does not apply to English paper piecing. Trying to fold and baste a 1/4" seam allowance over papers is tedious and the fabric tends to fray to nothing by the time you've finished. Instead, a seam allowance of approximately 3/8" is preferred but even this does not have to be too accurate.

1. When cutting multiple hexagons, stack up six or eight strips of fabric. Place one end on the rotating cutting mat. Place a hexagon paper on top (**Fig. 4**).

Fig. 4

2. Align the 3/8" line on the ruler with the edge of the paper hexagon **(Fig. 5)**. Cut the first side using a rotary cutter.

Fig. 5

3. Rotate the mat and align the ruler's 3/8" line with the next edge of paper hexagon. Cut second side **(Fig. 6)**. Repeat until all sides have been cut.

Fig. 6

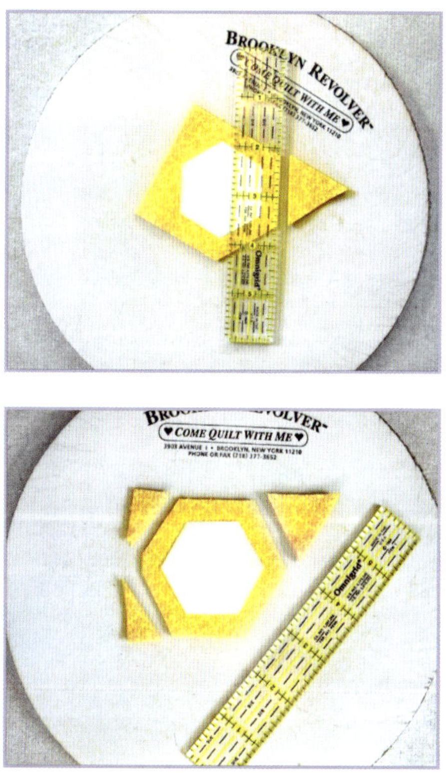

4. Move along the stack of fabric strips and continue cutting hexagons.

5. To speed cut hexagons from scraps or precuts, simply stack up scraps or precuts and rotary cut as previous.

6. Cut half hexagons in the same manner.

BASTING PAPERS TO FABRIC

English Paper Piecing is the perfect take-along project. Baste at the ballgame, in front of the TV, or even in the car. Keep a supply of papers and cut fabric shapes on hand in little zipper-top bags that you can grab for basting on the go.

Use a cotton basting thread; not only is it cheap and comes in large spools, but it breaks easily so it does not tug or pull when removing papers from a finished piece, and it is so soft that it won't mark fabric.

Use a size 8 betweens needle for basting. You may find a thimble helpful to push the needle through paper and fabric layers.

1. Place paper onto wrong side of fabric and place a pin in the center **(Fig. 7)**.

Fig. 7

2. Using basting thread with a large knot and starting with a straight of grain edge, fold fabric over paper edge so that it sits snugly against the paper. Take a stitch through both paper and fabric **(Fig. 8)**.

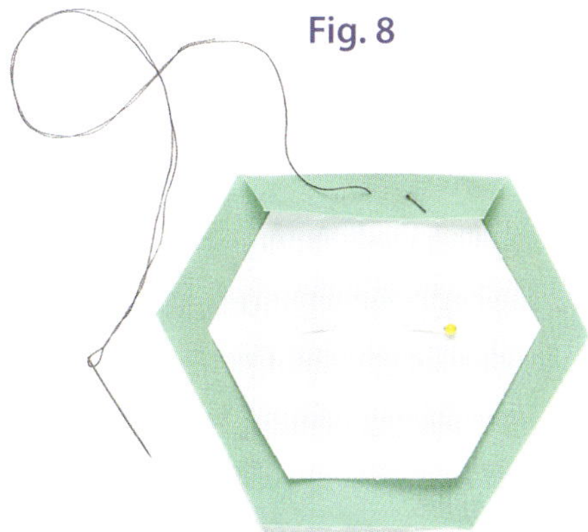

Fig. 8

3. Fold over next edge, forming a neat corner that is tight to the point of the paper. The heat from your fingers will keep the fold pressed in place. Take another stitch, catching in the corner fold **(Fig. 9)**.

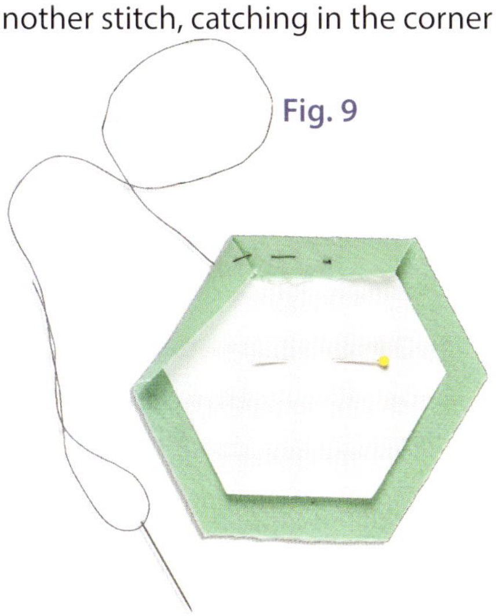

Fig. 9

4. Continue around the paper shape until back to the beginning knot **(Fig. 10)**. Take one backstitch to secure. Cut basting thread.

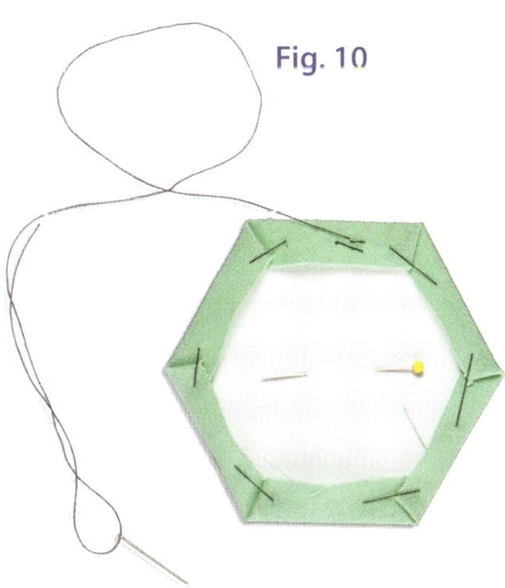

Fig. 10

KEEPING SEAMS ON THE STRAIGHT OF GRAIN

It is important to keep fabric edges on the straight of grain. However, when working with hexagons, four of the six straight edges are cut on the bias.

If you begin your basting on an edge that is cut on the straight of grain you know that the edge of the hexagon with the beginning and ending basting stitches is on the straight of grain. This gives you a quick reference point when looking to see which edge of the basted hexagon is on the straight of grain.

When whipstitching the hexagons together, keep all of those edges facing in the same directions (parallel to each other) and all of the grain lines will run in the same direction. Although this is not so important in the body of the project, it is essential at the outside of the project to avoid wavy edges, and it's a good habit to get into.

WHIPSTITCHING HEXAGONS TOGETHER

Use a thread with a polyester content, as 100% cotton thread is too soft and easily becomes worn and tangled. Use a size 8 betweens needle for whipstitching.

1. Hold two basted hexagons right sides together, matching shapes exactly. Starting with a knot, begin taking tiny whipstitches along folded fabric edges, avoiding the paper pieces inside **(Fig 11)**. Whipstitch two or three times at the end of the seam to anchor. Open out the two joined pieces **(Fig 12)**.

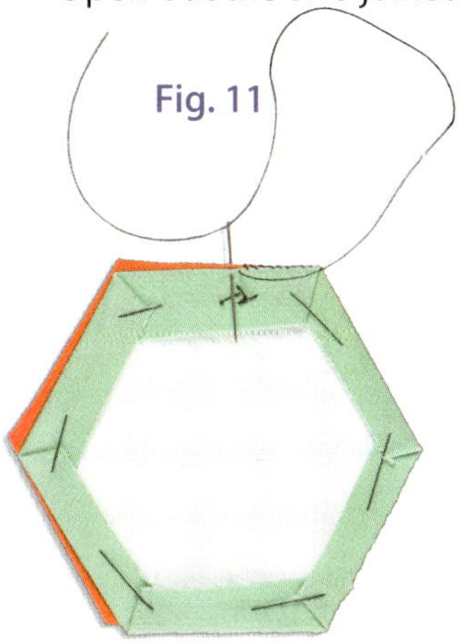

Fig. 11

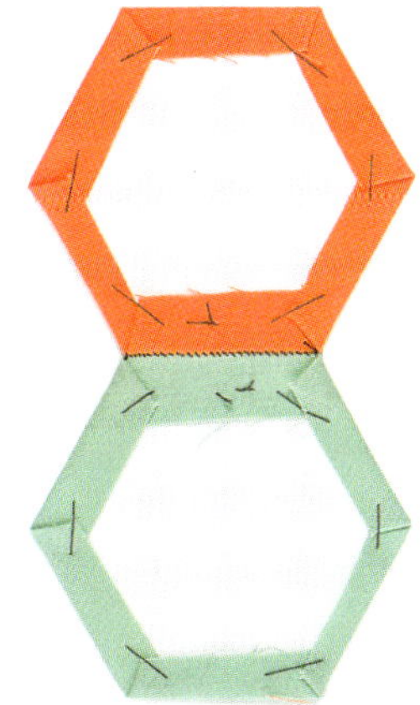

Fig. 12

2. To join next hexagon, match right sides and keep grainlines running parallel to whipstitch edges together **(Fig 13)**. Whipstitch two or three times at the end of the seam and cut thread.

Fig. 13

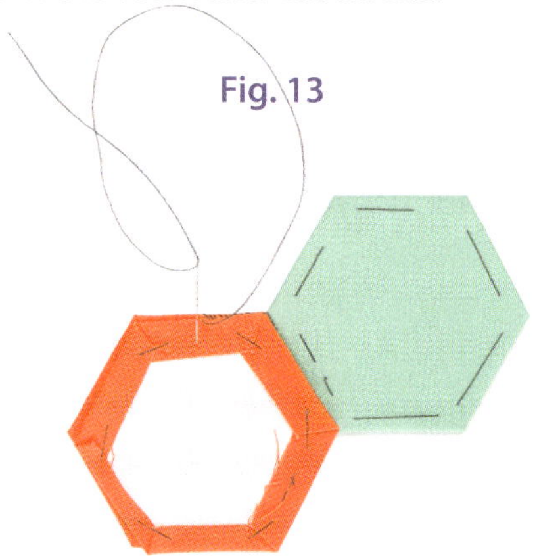

3. Open out the three joined pieces. Join the remaining seam in the same way as before **(Fig 14)** and then continue adding hexagons until the first hexagon is completely surrounded **(Fig 15)**.

Fig. 14

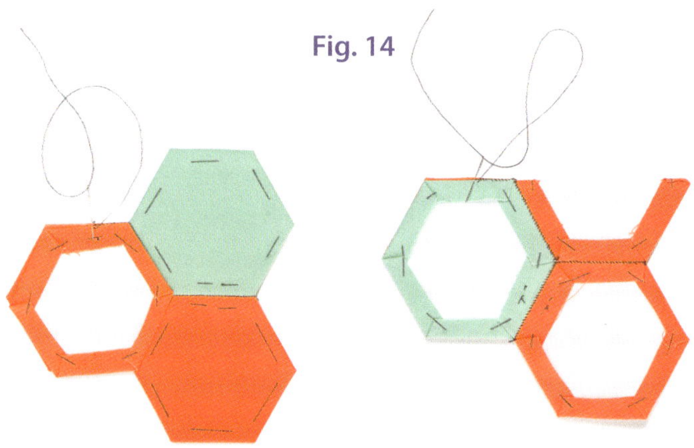

Fig. 15

REMOVING PAPER PIECES

Remove all papers prior to layering with batting and quilting. Papers can also be reused several times if the edges are still crisp. If you find your removed papers have a "nibbled" edge, your whipstitches are slightly too big and you are catching the edge of the paper in your stitching.

Do not remove a paper until that hexagon has been completely surrounded by other hexagons.

1. Using the points of small sharp scissors, undo the backstitch holding the basting in place. Continue around the hexagon, pulling out thread.

2. Bend one paper point slightly towards you. Use the point of the scissors to carefully pop out the paper. Iron papers flat to reuse.

No pressing is required during the construction of the project. As the basted pieces are whipstitched together and opened out, the seams will naturally lie flat, making opposing seams where three or more points come together. The only time it is necessary to press a completed project is when it is ready to be layered and quilted.

MACHINE PIECING AND SEWING

Precise cutting, followed by accurate piecing or sewing, will ensure that all pieces fit together well.

- Set sewing machine stitch length for approximately 11 stitches per inch.

- Use neutral-colored general-purpose sewing thread (not quilting thread) in needle and in bobbin.

- An accurate seam allowance is essential. Seam allowances are 1/4" unless otherwise indicated. Presser feet that are 1/4" wide are available for most sewing machines.

- When piecing or sewing, always place pieces right sides together and match raw edges unless otherwise indicated; pin if necessary.

- Chain piecing saves time and will usually result in more accurate piecing.

- Trim away points of seam allowances that extend beyond edges of sewn pieces.

SEWING ACROSS SEAM INTERSECTIONS

When sewing across intersection of two seams, place pieces right sides together and match seams exactly, making sure seam allowances are pressed in opposite directions (**Fig. 16**).

Fig. 16

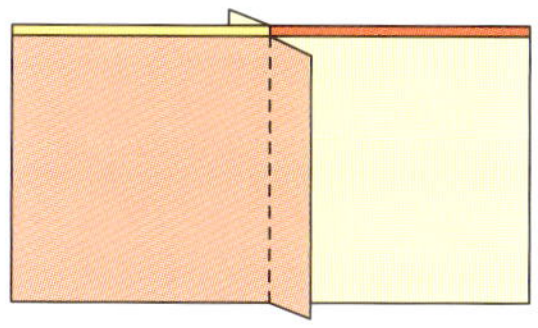

SEWING SHARP POINTS

To ensure sharp points when joining triangular or diagonal pieces, stitch across the center of the "X" (shown in pink) formed on wrong side by previous seams (**Fig. 17**).

Fig. 17

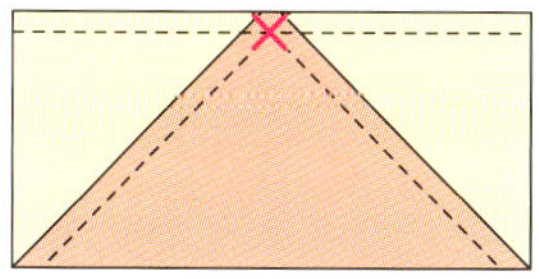

PRESSING

- Use steam iron set on "Cotton" for pressing cotton fabrics or "Linen" for pressing linen fabrics.

- Press after sewing each seam.

- Seam allowances are almost always pressed to one side, usually toward darker fabric. However, to reduce bulk it may occasionally be necessary to press seam allowances toward the lighter fabric or even to press them open.

- To prevent dark fabric seam allowance from showing through light fabric, trim darker seam allowance slightly narrower than lighter seam allowance.

- To press long seams, such as those in long strip sets, without curving or other distortion, lay strips across width of the ironing board.

- When sewing blocks into rows, seam allowances may be pressed in one direction in odd numbered rows and in the opposite direction in even numbered rows. When sewing rows together, press seam allowances in one direction.

ADDING MITERED BORDERS

Instructions are given for adding mitered borders to a quilt top center. The same instructions apply when making the **Floral Appliqué Pillow**, page 22.

1. Mark the center of each edge of quilt top.

2. Mark center of one long edge of top border. Measure across center of quilt top. Matching center marks and raw edges, pin border to center of quilt top edge. From center of border, measure out 1/2 the width of the quilt top in both directions and mark. Match marks on border with corners of quilt top and pin. Easing in any fullness, pin border to quilt top between center and corners. Sew border to quilt top, beginning and ending seams exactly 1/4" from each corner of quilt top and backstitching at beginning and end of stitching. **(Fig. 18)**.

Fig. 18

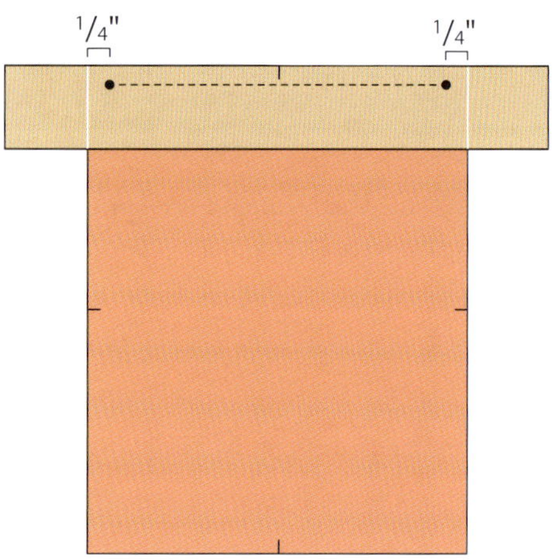

3. Repeat Step 2 to sew bottom, then side borders, to center section of quilt top. To temporarily move first two borders out of the way, fold and pin ends as shown in **Fig. 19**.

Fig. 19

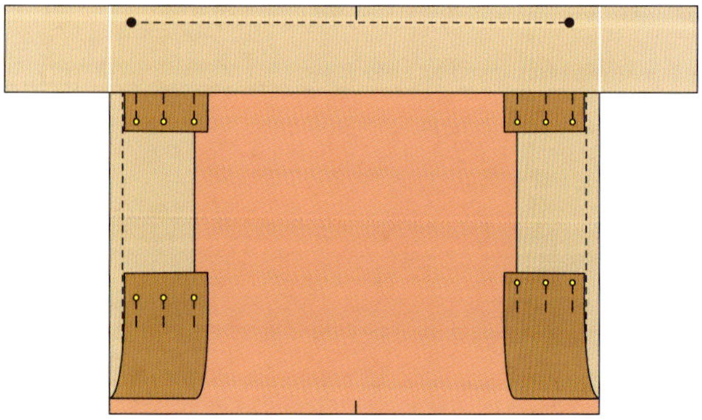

4. Fold one corner of the quilt top diagonally with right sides together; use rotary cutting ruler to mark stitching line as shown in **Fig. 20**. Pin strips together along drawn line. Sew on drawn line, backstitching at beginning and end of stitching **(Fig. 21)**.

Fig. 20

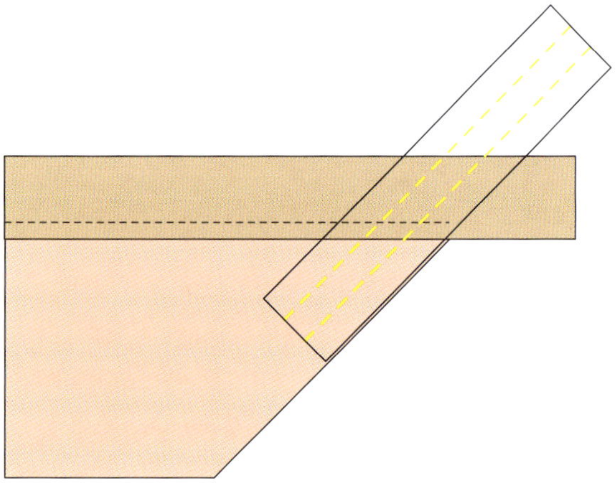

Fig. 21

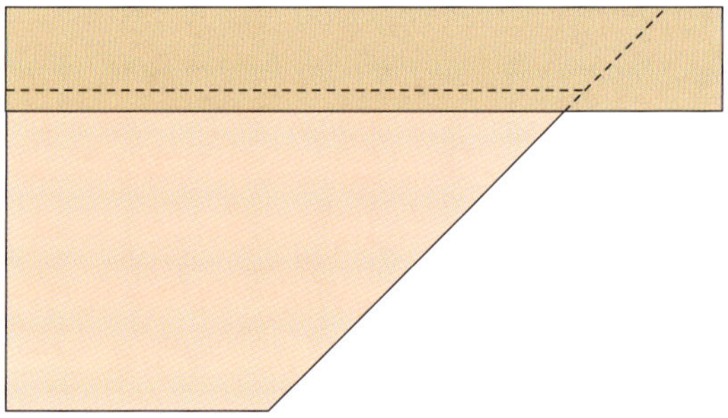

5. Turn mitered corner right side up. Check to see that there is not a gap at the inner end of the seam and that the corner does not pucker.

6. Trim seam allowances to 1/4"; press to one side.

7. Repeat Steps 4-6 to miter each remaining corner.

APPLIQUÉ

PREPARING FUSIBLE APPLIQUÉS

White or light-colored fabrics may need to be lined with fusible interfacing before applying fusible web to prevent darker fabrics from showing through.

1. Place paper-backed fusible web, paper side up, over appliqué pattern. Trace pattern onto paper side of web with pencil as many times as indicated in project instructions for a single fabric.

2. Rough-cut the patterns apart about 1/2" **outside** the traced lines.

3. Cut into the traced line to cut away the center of the fusible web 1/4" **inside** the traced line **(Fig. 22)**. Do not cut on the line. It may not be necessary to cut away the center of small or narrow pieces.

Fig. 22

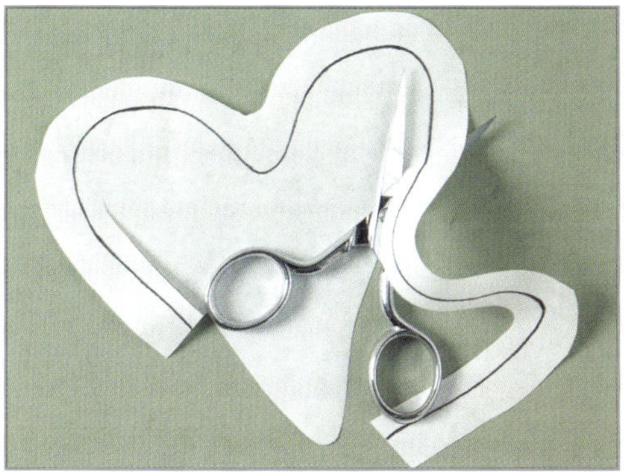

4. Follow manufacturer's instructions to fuse traced patterns to wrong side of fabrics **(Fig. 23)**. Do not remove paper backing.

Fig. 23

5. Use scissors to cut out appliqué pieces **on** traced lines. Remove paper backing from all pieces.

QUILTING

Quilting holds the three layers (top, batting, and backing) of the quilt together and can be done by hand or machine. Because marking, layering, and quilting are interrelated and may be done in different orders depending on circumstances, please read entire Quilting section, pages 49-52, before beginning project.

MARKING QUILTING LINES

Quilting lines may be marked using fabric marking pencils, chalk markers, or water- or air-soluble pens.

Simple quilting designs may be marked with chalk or chalk pencil after basting. A small area may be marked, then quilted, before moving to next area to be marked. Intricate designs should be marked before basting using a more durable marker.

Caution: Pressing may permanently set some marks. Test different markers on scrap fabric to find one that marks clearly and can be thoroughly removed.

A wide variety of pre-cut quilting stencils, as well as entire books of quilting patterns, are available. Using a stencil makes it easier to mark intricate or repetitive designs.

To make a stencil from a pattern, center template plastic over pattern and use a permanent marker to trace pattern onto plastic. Use a craft knife with single or double blade to cut channels along traced lines **(Fig. 24)**.

Fig. 24

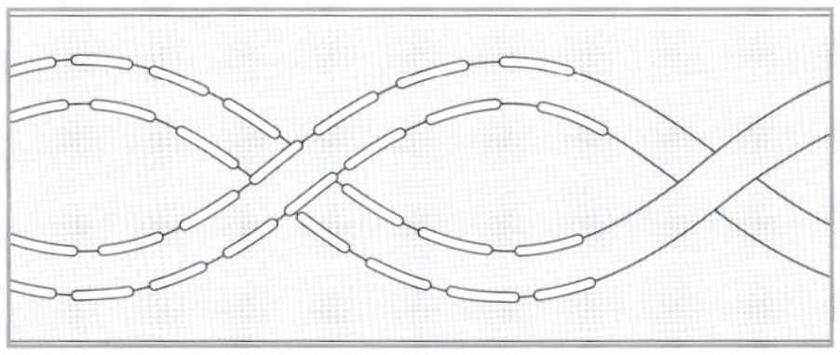

PREPARING THE BACKING

To allow for slight shifting of quilt top during quilting, backing should be approximately 4" larger on all sides for quilts and 2" larger on all sides for smaller projects. Yardage requirements listed for quilt backings are calculated for 43"/44"w fabric. Using 90"w or 108"w fabric for the backing of a bed-sized quilt may eliminate piecing. To piece a backing using 43"/44"w fabric, use the following instructions.

1. Measure length and width of quilt top; add 8" (4") to each measurement.

2. If determined width is 79" or less, cut backing fabric into two lengths slightly longer than determined length measurement. Trim selvages. Place lengths with right sides facing and sew long edges together, forming tube **(Fig. 25)**. Match seams and press along one fold **(Fig. 26)**. Cut along pressed fold to form single piece **(Fig. 27)**.

Fig. 25

Fig. 26

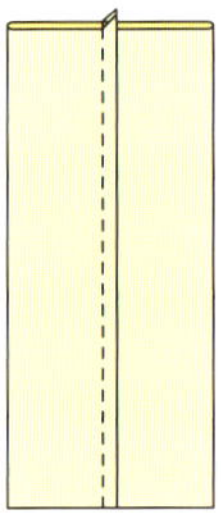

Fig. 27

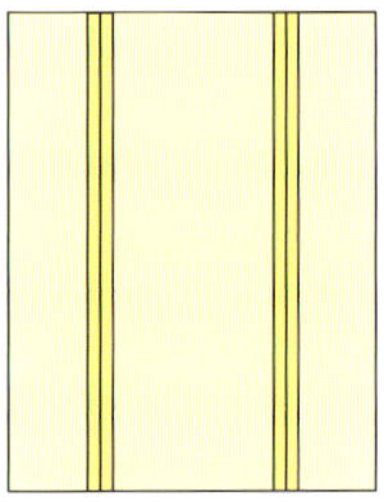

3. If determined width is more than 79", it may require less fabric yardage if the backing is pieced horizontally. Divide determined length measurement by 40" to determine how many widths will be needed. Cut required number of widths the determined width measurement. Trim selvages. Sew long edges together to form single piece.

4. Trim backing to size determined in Step 1; press seam allowances open.

CHOOSING THE BATTING

The appropriate batting will make quilting easier. For fine hand quilting, choose low-loft batting. All cotton or cotton/polyester blend battings work well for machine quilting because the cotton helps "grip" quilt layers. If quilt is to be tied, a high-loft batting, sometimes called extra-loft or fat batting, may be used to make quilt "fluffy."

Types of batting include cotton, polyester, wool, cotton/polyester blend, cotton/wool blend, and silk.

When selecting batting, refer to package labels for characteristics and care instructions. Cut batting same size as prepared backing.

ASSEMBLING THE QUILT

1. Examine wrong side of quilt top closely; trim any seam allowances and clip any threads that may show through front of the quilt. Press quilt top, being careful not to "set" any marked quilting lines.

2. Place backing wrong side up on flat surface. Use masking tape to tape edges of backing to surface. Place batting on top of backing fabric. Smooth batting gently, being careful not to stretch or tear. Center quilt top right side up on batting.

3. Use 1" rustproof safety pins to "pin-baste" all layers together, spacing pins approximately 4" apart. Begin at center and work toward outer edges to secure all layers. If possible, place pins away from areas that will be quilted, although pins may be removed as needed when quilting.

HAND QUILTING

The quilting stitch is a basic Running Stitch, page 55, that forms a broken line on the quilt top and backing. Stitches on the quilt top and backing should be straight and equal in length.

1. Secure center of quilt in hoop or frame. Check quilt top and backing to make sure they are smooth. Always begin quilting in the center of the quilt and work toward the outside edges.

2. Thread needle with an 18" - 20" length of quilting thread; knot one end. Using a thimble, insert needle into quilt top and batting approximately $^1/_2$" from where you wish to begin (**Fig. 28**); when knot catches on quilt top, give thread a quick, short pull to "pop" knot through fabric into batting (**Fig. 29**).

Fig. 28

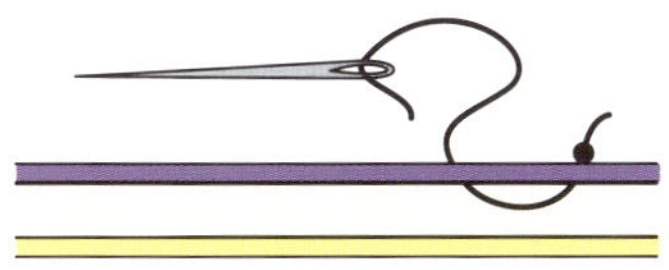

Fig. 29

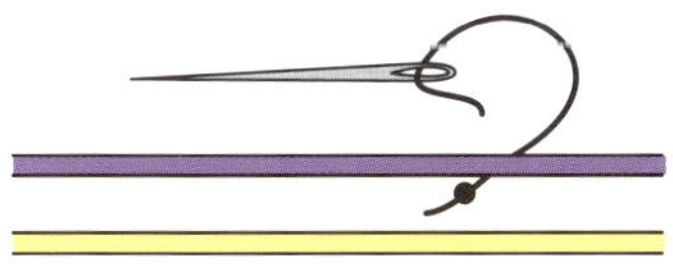

3. Holding the needle with your sewing hand and placing your other hand underneath the quilt, use thimble to push the tip of the needle down through all layers. As soon as needle touches your finger underneath, use that finger to push the tip of the needle only back up through the layers to top of quilt. (The amount of the needle showing above the fabric determines the length of the quilting stitch.) Referring to **Fig. 30**, rock the needle up and down, taking three to six stitches before bringing the needle and thread completely through the layers. Check the back of the quilt to make sure stitches are going through all layers. When quilting through a seam allowance or quilting a curve or corner, you may need to make one stitch at a time.

Fig. 30

4. When you reach the end of your thread, knot thread close to the fabric and "pop" knot into batting; clip thread close to fabric.
5. Stop and move your hoop as often as necessary. You do not have to tie a knot every time you move your hoop; you may leave the thread dangling and pick it up again when you return to that part of the quilt.

MACHINE QUILTING METHODS

Use general-purpose thread in bobbin. Do not use quilting thread. Thread the needle of machine with general-purpose thread or transparent monofilament thread to make quilting blend with quilt top fabrics. Use decorative thread, such as a metallic or contrasting-color general-purpose thread, to make quilting lines stand out more.

Straight-Line Quilting

The term "straight-line" is somewhat deceptive, since curves (especially gentle ones) as well as straight lines can be stitched with this technique.

1. Set stitch length for six to ten stitches per inch and attach walking foot to sewing machine.

2. Determine which section of quilt will have longest continuous quilting line, often the area from center top to center bottom. Roll up and secure each edge of quilt to help reduce the bulk, keeping fabrics smooth. Smaller projects may not need to be rolled.

3. Begin stitching on longest quilting line, using very short stitches for the first $^1/_4$" to "lock" quilting. Stitch across project, using one hand on each side of walking foot to slightly spread fabric and to guide fabric through machine. Lock stitches at end of quilting line.
4. Continue machine quilting, stitching longer quilting lines first to stabilize quilt before moving on to other areas.

Free-Motion Quilting

Free-motion quilting may be free form or may follow a marked pattern.

1. Attach darning foot to sewing machine and lower or cover feed dogs.

2. Position quilt under darning foot; lower foot. Holding top thread, take a stitch and pull bobbin thread to top of quilt. To "lock" beginning of quilting line, hold top and bobbin threads while making three to five stitches in place.

3. Use one hand on each side of darning foot to slightly spread fabric and to move fabric through the machine. Even stitch length is achieved by using smooth, flowing hand motion and steady machine speed. Slow machine speed and fast hand movement will create long stitches. Fast machine speed and slow hand movement will create short stitches. Move quilt sideways, back and forth, in a circular motion, or in a random motion to create desired designs; do not rotate quilt. Lock stitches at end of each quilting line.

BINDING

MAKING CONTINUOUS BIAS BINDING

1. Cut a square from binding fabric the size indicated in the project instructions. Cut square in half diagonally to make two triangles.

2. With right sides together and using a $^1/_4$" seam allowance, sew triangles together (**Fig. 31**); press seam allowance open.

Fig. 31

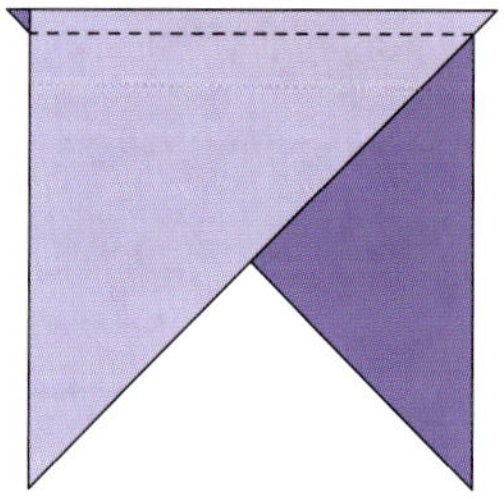

3. On wrong side of fabric, draw lines the width of the binding as specified in the project instructions, usually $2^1/_4$" (**Fig. 32**). Cut off any remaining fabric less than this width.

Fig. 32

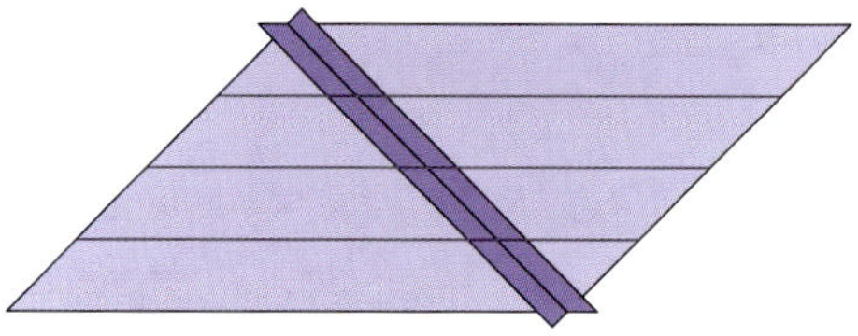

4. With right sides inside, bring short edges together to form a tube; match raw edges so that first drawn line of top section meets second drawn line of bottom section (**Fig. 33**).

Fig. 33

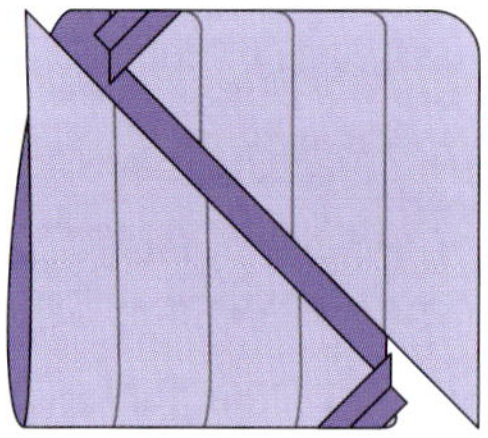

5. Carefully pin edges together by inserting pins through drawn lines at the point where drawn lines intersect, making sure the pins go through intersections on both sides. Using a $^1/_4$" seam allowance, sew edges together. Press seam allowance open.

6. To cut continuous strip, begin cutting along first drawn line (**Fig. 34**). Continue cutting along drawn line around tube.

Fig. 34

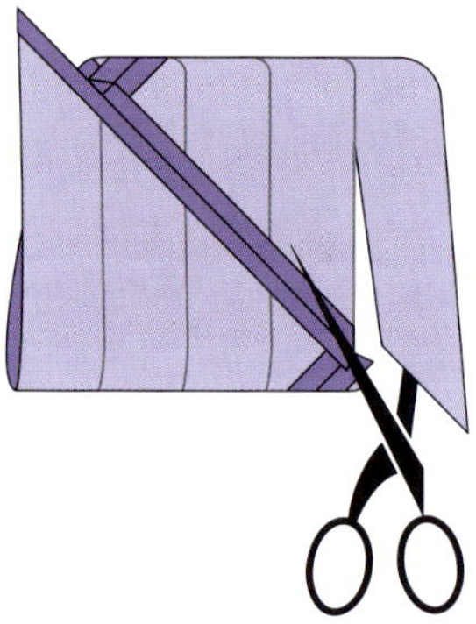

7. Trim ends of bias strip square.

8. Matching wrong sides and raw edges, press bias strip in half lengthwise to complete binding.

ATTACHING BINDING WITH MITERED CORNERS

1. Beginning with one end near center on bottom edge of quilt, lay binding around quilt to make sure that seams in binding will not end up at a corner. Adjust placement if necessary. Matching raw edges of binding to raw edge of quilt top, pin binding to right side of quilt along one edge.

2. When you reach first corner, mark $^{1}/_{4}$" from corner of quilt top **(Fig. 35)**.

Fig. 35

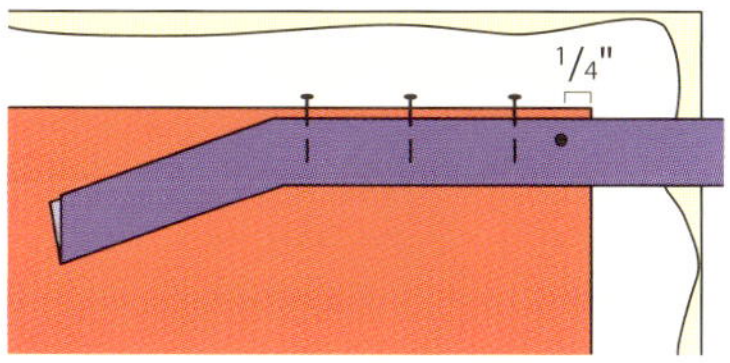

3. Beginning approximately 10" from end of binding and using a $^{1}/_{4}$" seam allowance, sew binding to quilt, backstitching at beginning of stitching and at mark **(Fig. 36)**. Lift needle out of fabric and clip thread.

Fig. 36

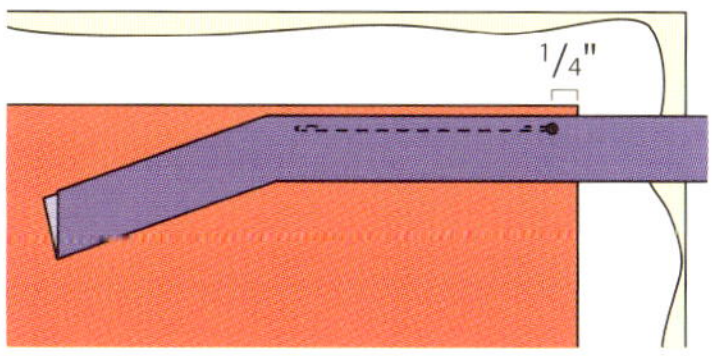

4. Fold binding as shown in **Figs. 37-38** and pin binding to adjacent side, matching raw edges. When you've reached the next corner, mark $^{1}/_{4}$" from edge of quilt top.

Fig. 37

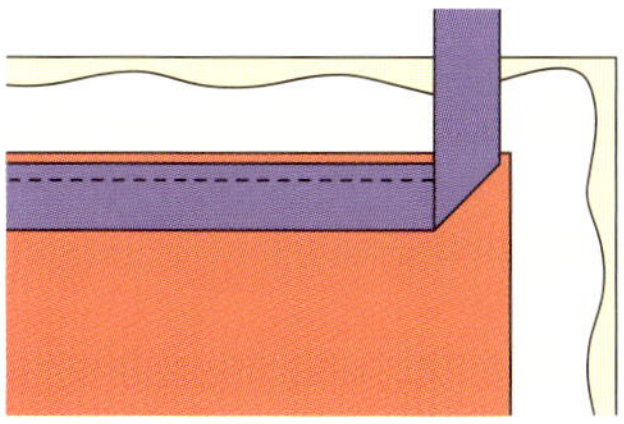

Fig. 38

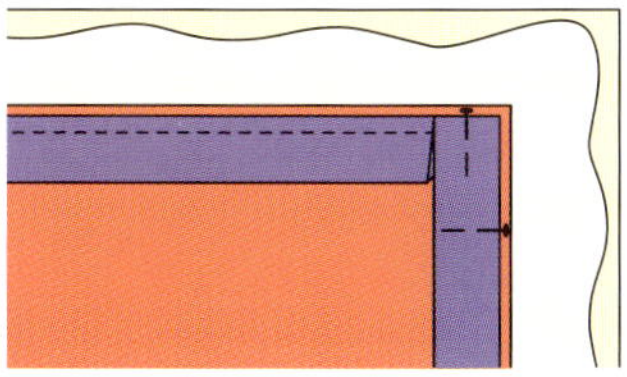

5. Backstitching at edge of quilt top, sew pinned binding to quilt **(Fig. 39)**; backstitch at the next mark. Lift needle out of fabric and clip thread.

Fig. 39

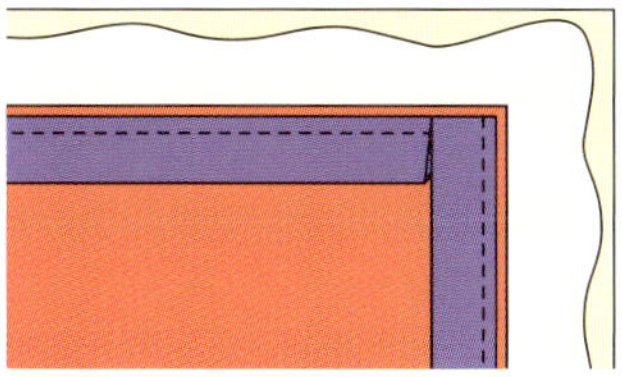

6. Continue sewing binding to quilt, stopping approximately 10" from starting point **(Fig. 40)**.

Fig. 40

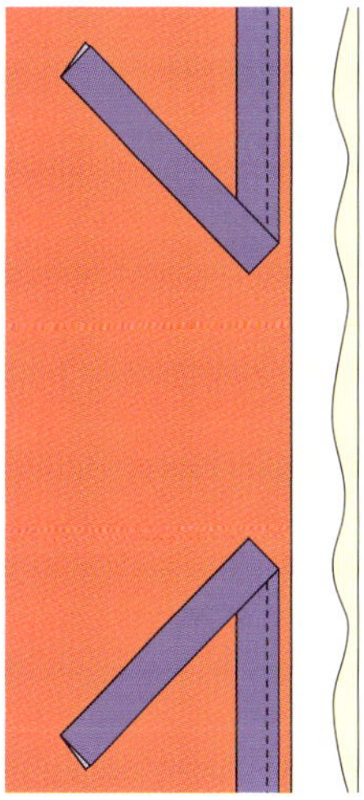

7. Bring beginning and end of binding to center of opening and fold each end back, leaving a 1/4" space between folds **(Fig. 41)**. Finger press folds.

Fig. 41

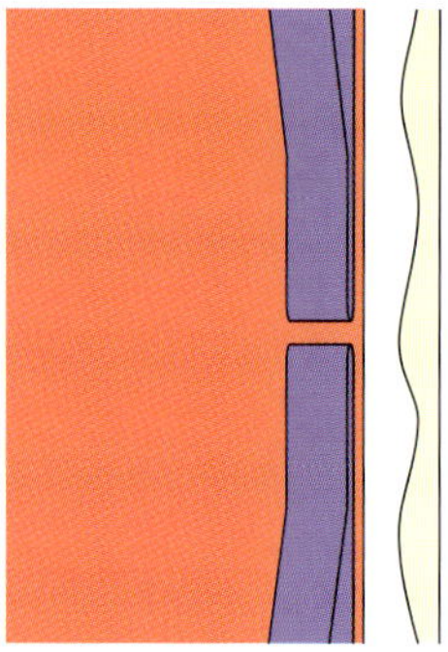

8. Unfold ends of binding and draw a line across wrong side in finger-pressed crease. Draw a line through the lengthwise pressed fold of binding at the same spot to create a cross mark. With edge of ruler at cross mark, line up 45° angle marking on ruler with one long side of binding. Draw a diagonal line from edge to edge. Repeat on remaining end, making sure that the two diagonal lines are angled the same way **(Fig. 42)**.

Fig. 42

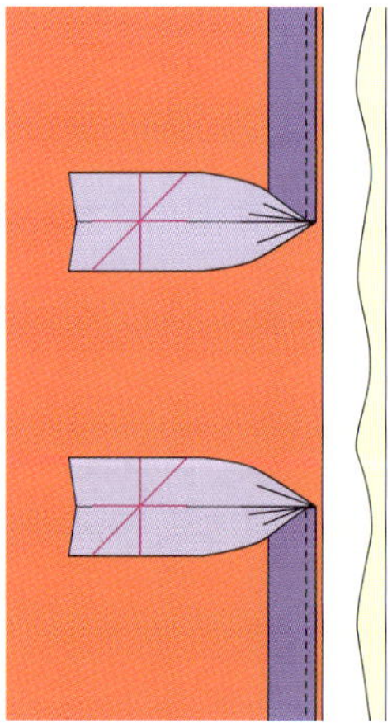

9. Matching right sides and diagonal lines, pin binding ends together at right angles **(Fig. 43)**.

Fig. 43

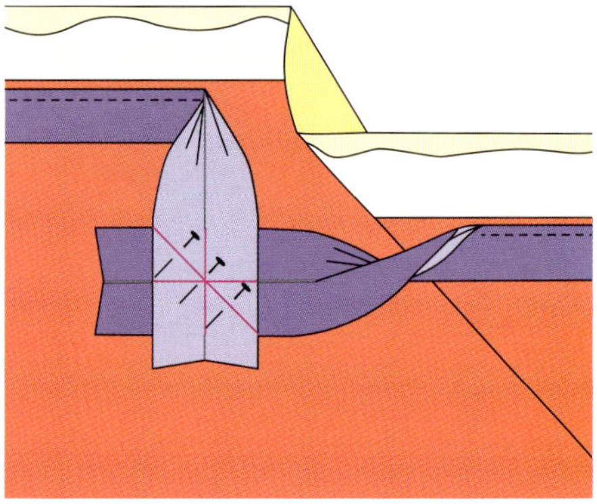

10. Machine stitch along diagonal line **(Fig. 44)**, removing pins as you stitch.

Fig. 44

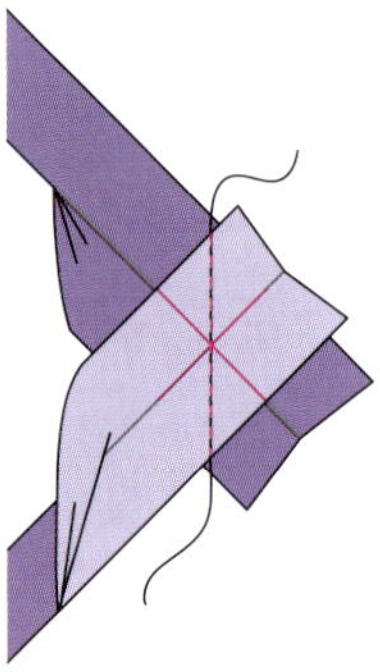

11. Lay binding against quilt to double check that it is correct length.

12. Trim binding ends, leaving 1/4" seam allowance; press seam open. Stitch binding to quilt.

13. Trim backing and batting even with edges of quilt top.

14. On one edge of quilt, fold binding over to quilt backing and pin pressed edge in place, covering stitching line (**Fig. 45**). On adjacent side, fold binding over, forming a mitered corner (**Fig. 46**). Repeat to pin remainder of binding in place.

Fig. 45

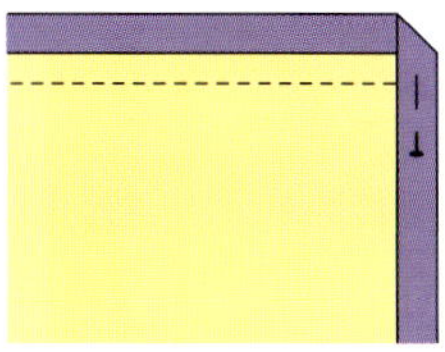

Fig. 46

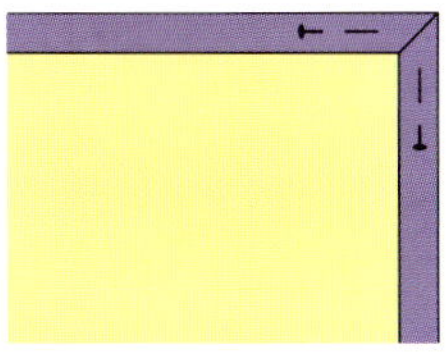

15. Blindstitch binding to backing, taking care not to stitch through to front of quilt.

HAND STITCHES

BLIND STITCH

Come up at 1. Go down at 2 and come up at 3. The length of stitches may be varied as desired (**Fig. 47**).

Fig. 47

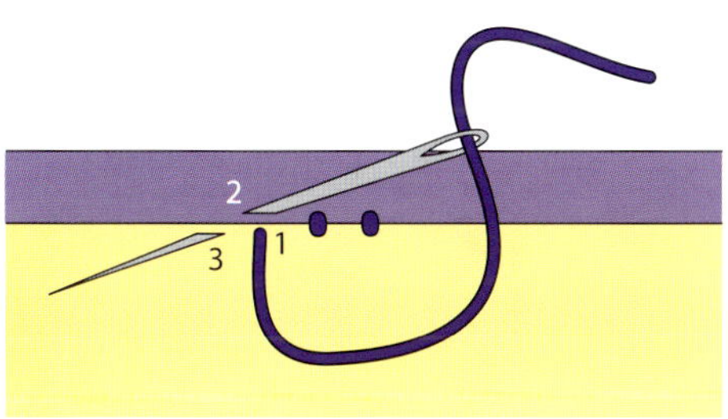

BUTTONHOLE STITCH

Come up at 1. Go down at 2 and come up at 3, keeping thread below point of needle (**Fig. 48**). Continue working as shown in **Fig. 49**.

Fig. 48

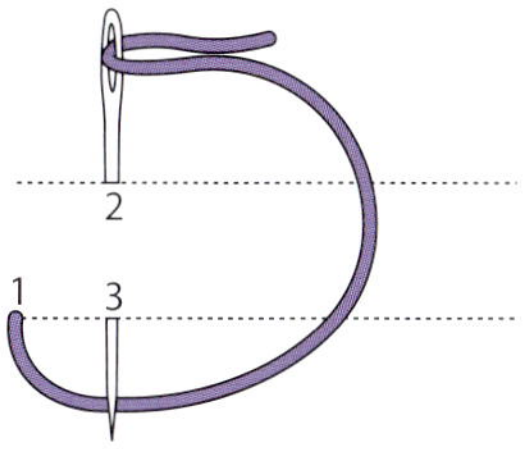

Fig. 49

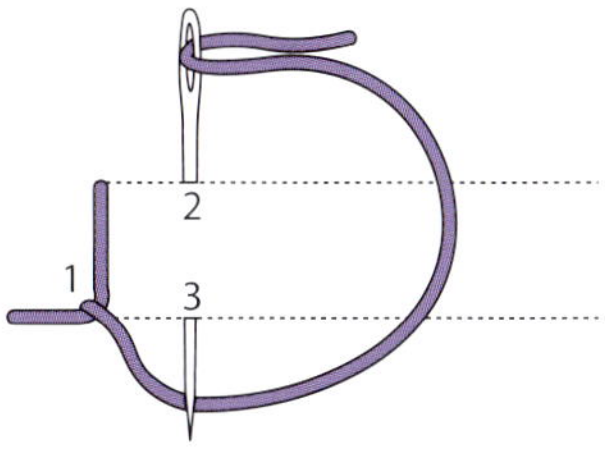

OUTLINE STITCH

Come up at 1. Keeping thread above the stitching line, go down at 2 and come up at 3. Go down at 4 and come up at 5 (**Fig. 50**).

Fig. 50

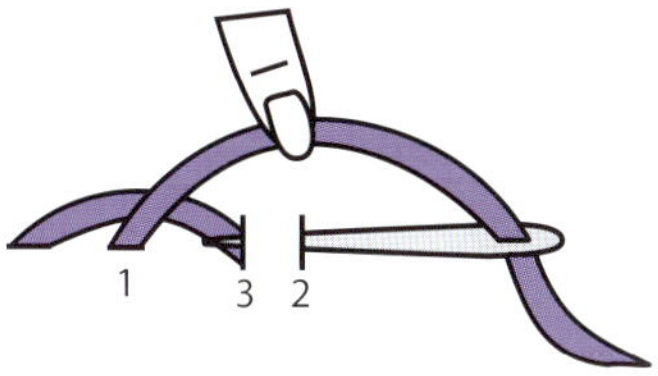

RUNNING STITCH

The Running Stitch consists of a series of straight stitches with the stitch length equal to the space between stitches. Come up at 1, go down at 2, and come up at 3 (**Fig. 51**).

Fig. 51

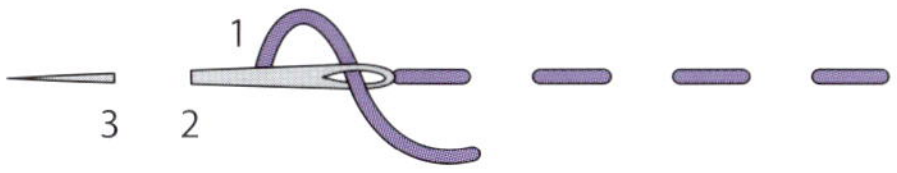

WHIPSTITCH

Come up at 1. Go down at 2, directly across from 1 (**Fig. 52**). Come up at 3, approximately $^{1}/_{16}$" below 1. Continue working in the same manner, coming up at odd numbers and going down at even numbers.

Fig. 52

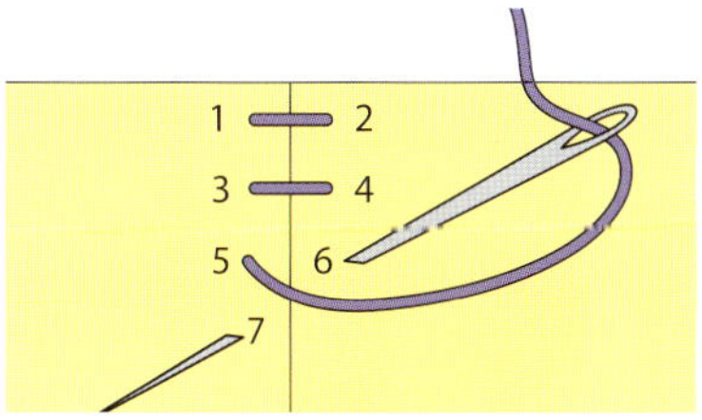

Meet The Designer:

Rebekah Shucksmith

Rebekah Shucksmith has a life-long connection to English paper piecing.

"I was fortunate enough to have a mother who taught me how to sew, crochet, and knit before I was even old enough to read," Rebekah says. "Being British, English paper piecing was the only way I knew how to make a quilt, so I have more than 30 years experience in this technique."

A resident of the United States since 2002, Rebekah teaches English paper piecing, hand embroidery, and hand buttonhole stitch appliqué at quilt guild workshops and quilt stores. "I believe that there is a movement to return to handmade heirloom quality projects," she says, "I am proud to be passing on these long-forgotten skills to a new generation. I love that I can take a handful of old scraps and make a quilt with nothing more than a needle and thread, no electricity required!"

Her design style is "everything vintage," she says. "I have a huge stash of original feed sacks and fabrics from the 1930s which I sprinkle into my quilts for authenticity. This particular book was inspired by a trip to the seaside in Cape May, New Jersey, where I was inspired by the abundance of summer flowers, the striped awnings, and the old-fashioned candy stores, to create this vintage beach cottage collection."

Rebekah lives with her young son, Archie, in upstate New York, where she works part time in an old-fashioned 60-year-old bookstore. *Salt Water Taffy Collection* is her first book for Leisure Arts.

Many thanks to Cindy Dunlap of Sew It Is for her beautiful longarm machine quilting. www.sewitis.com

Thank you to Bellwether Dry Goods for their heirloom quality hand quilting. www.bellwetherdrygoods.com

Thanks to www.paperpieces.com for their huge selection of paper pieces in every shape and size imaginable.

Production Team: Technical Editor – Lisa Lancaster; Associate Editor – Jean Lewis; Editorial Writer – Susan Frantz Wiles; Art Category Manager – Lora Puls; Graphic Artists – Leia Morshedi and Kytanna McFarlin; Photography Stylist – Lori Wenger; Photographer – Jason Masters